The Psychology of Murder

Stuart Palmer

The Psychology
of Murder

Thomas Y. Crowell Company

New York · Established 1834

To Anne

Author's Note

THE CO-OPERATION of many people is necessary in order to carry out a research project such as the one reported here. I wish especially to express my appreciation to the following:

Dr. William F. Bugden   Mr. John L. McGillen
Professor Owen B. Durgin   Dr. Norman A. Neiberg
Mrs. Harold Eastman   Dr. Melville Nielson
Dr. Raymond R. Gilbert   Warden Allen L. Robbins
Warden Parker L. Hancock   Mrs. Richard Roy
Miss Helen F. Jenkins   Mr. John N. Sanborn
Miss Janet LaChance   Dr. J. Gordon Shaw
Mr. Harold V. Langlois   Mr. Thomas Worth

I should like also to thank my wife, Anne S. Palmer, for her understanding help. And, perhaps most of all, I thank the fifty-one men convicted of murder, their mothers, and other relatives whose lives form the raw material of this book.

Two sections of this book were written by Joseph T. Galvin and one section by Raymond V. Peters. Mr. Galvin is serving a life sentence for murder. He has continually proclaimed his innocence. Mr. Peters served twenty years of a life sentence for murder and was conditionally pardoned in July, 1958.

A number of case studies, some of which are not part of the group of fifty-one, are presented. Minor details have been changed in order to protect the guilty—as well as the innocent. However, every effort has been made to retain the original meanings of the data.

It should be noted also that this research was financed partially by grants from the Central University Research Fund of the University of New Hampshire.

STUART PALMER

Contents

Contents

The Psychology of Murder

1.   Background of the Study

T HIS BOOK tells of a study of fifty-one men convicted of murder, of their early life experiences, and of how those experiences led each of them to kill one or more of their fellow human beings. The study was carried out in New England over a period of three years, 1956 to 1959. During that time, and following a careful plan, I interviewed murderers, their relatives and friends, and correctional officials.

A control group of fifty-one men who had not committed murder was used in order to have a standard with which to compare the murderers. This control group was composed of the nearest-in-age brother of each murderer. In the research, special emphasis was placed on finding out whether there was a connection between severe frustration experienced in infancy and childhood and murder committed in adolescence or adulthood. However, many other aspects of the total problem of murder were also investigated and will be reported on here.

By almost any set of standards murder is one of the most aggressive, violent, and antisocial acts which a human being can commit. Most, if not all, societies have strong taboos against indiscriminate, purposeful killing of their members except under very special circumstances. Yet, murder flourishes. Each year in this country at least seven thousand murders are committed.[1] Why is this? What are the influences which drive some human beings to kill others? As William A. White has said, "Behind every crime lies a secret." What are the "secrets" behind crimes of murder? Is there a general "secret" behind all, or most, cases of murder?

This book attempts to throw a clear light on these questions. It attempts to provide some answers to the apparent riddles behind murders of various kinds. Although the book is essentially a scientific report, the presentation is directed toward the intelligent layman who has an interest in crime and the criminal, as well as toward behavioral scientists and penologists. Therefore, I have tried to avoid the use of sociological and psychological jargon insofar as possible. I trust specialists will find the report of value. But it is also my hope that the book will reach a wider audience. For if crime, murder in particular, is to be reduced, there must be increased understanding on the parts of nonprofessionals as well as professionals concerning the influences that lie behind it. In one way or another, we are all involved in problems of crime and we must all share in any effective elimination of it.

This chapter presents general background material concerning murder and tells of the particular research problems involved in the study. Also, the procedures used to gather the information are explained. The next four chapters present the findings of the research. The numerical results are illustrated with actual statements by the murderers and by others. In the final chapter, the results are summarized and possible ways of decreasing the murder rate and of rehabilitating murderers are outlined.

Most chapters are followed by extended case studies which are meant to illuminate the concerns of the given chapters. The aim throughout has been to blend theory, basic findings, and true life stories so that each gives meaning to the others. Statistical material has been kept to a minimum. Professionals should consult the tables in Appendix A for added detail.

Contrary to fairly widespread belief, murder and homicide are not necessarily synonymous. Homicide is the larger category and includes justifiable, legal killing as well as murder and manslaughter. A police officer who shoots and kills an escaping convict is committing justifiable homicide. Likewise, a man who protects his family and home by killing a burglar is considered to have committed justifiable homicide.

With respect to nonjustifiable homicide—murder and manslaughter—state laws vary widely. The general consensus is that murder in the first degree is premeditated, intentional, and malicious killing. The killing committed during an armed robbery is usually a clear-cut case of first-degree murder. Murder in the second degree is much the same as in the first degree except that the killing is usually considered to be somewhat less premeditated and malicious. For example, the parent who grows angry at his child, loses control of himself, and kills the child is likely to be convicted of second-degree murder. (Legally, there is some premeditation here.)

Manslaughter is usually defined as unpremeditated yet to some degree malicious killing. In first-degree manslaughter,[2] the state laws frequently specify that the victim must have provoked the killer to some extent. Cases where two men get in an argument, one threatens the other, and the latter kills the one who threatened him are often considered manslaughter of the first degree. In second-degree manslaughter,[3] the killing is considered to have been only indirectly intentional and malicious; a typical example here would be the man who has had a number of drinks, drives his car, and kills a pedestrian.

In this book, first- and second-degree murder and first-degree manslaughter will all be treated as murder. The line between murder and manslaughter is, in practice, a changing and unrealistic one. After all, who is to say whether a killing was premeditated? Often the killer himself does not know. The killing may have been unconsciously premeditated or not premeditated at all. Again, who is to say whether the killer was provoked by the victim? Was he provoked just prior to the crime, a year before, several times, never? Further, second-degree murder charges are frequently reduced to first-degree manslaughter charges when the defendant agrees to plead guilty. On the other hand, second-degree manslaughter, which is usually sheer negligence on the part of the killer, is quite different from murder and so is not treated synonymously with the latter here.

Sentences for these forms of nonjustifiable homicide also vary from state to state. The penalty for first-degree murder is either death or life imprisonment. For second-degree murder the penalty may be a number of years of imprisonment, usually varying from twenty to life. For first-degree manslaughter the length of imprisonment is usually around fifteen years.

Murder rates are generally expressed as so many murders (and first-degree manslaughters) per 100,000 of the population. In the United States during the year 1957 there occurred an estimated 6,920 murders [4] while the total resident population was judged to be about 169,382,000.[5] Therefore, the known murder rate was approximately 4.1. Of course, some murders are committed and are never legally recognized as such. Frequently this is because the judgment of the coroner or physician is in error, although it may be because the death of the victim is never officially reported. There is no way of estimating closely how many of these unknown murders are committed, but the figure for the United States is probably several thousand per year.

Traditionally, known murder rates have been higher in the southern states than in any other region of the United States. In 1957, the urban murder rate in the "east south central" states of Alabama, Kentucky, Mississippi, and Tennessee was 12.6 per 100,000 of the population. This was nine times as high as in the New England states, which had a rate of 1.4—the lowest rate. Alabama had the highest urban rate of any state, 16.2, while New Hampshire had the lowest, 0.4. That is, there was forty times as much urban murder in Alabama as in New Hampshire, allowing for population differences.[6]

The high murder rate in the south is partially accounted for by the fact that known murder rates are much higher among Negroes than whites.[7] This is not to say that Negroes are innately more vicious than whites. Rather, the difference is probably explained on the basis that social pressures on Negroes are greater than on whites and that, because of prejudice, Negroes are more often convicted, other things being equal.

The United States has one of the highest murder rates in the world. Ceylon and the Italian provinces of Sardinia, Sicily,

4

and Calabria are among the few places where the rate is higher. On the other hand, Iceland, a relatively modern country with a population of slightly over 150,000, has an exceedingly low rate for murder and other crimes. During the past few centuries, there has been no killing in Iceland which is definitely known to have been murder.[8] Why are there these differences? I think the study reported here will shed some light on this question.

In the United States and in most other modern countries, large cities tend to have higher murder rates than small cities and rural places. This might well be due to the anxieties of urban living and the fact that those rural dwellers who are most maladjusted frequently move to the large cities. Another point: in the United States, men commit four to five times as much known murder as do women.[9] In all probability, this is partially explained by the fact that in most groups more emphasis is placed on training the female child to follow the acceptable patterns of behavior than is the case with the male child. Also, the female's role generally allows for less experience with the weapons of murder than does the role of the male.

While the over-all known felony crime rate in the United States has increased considerably in recent years, the known murder rate has decreased slightly.[10] With respect to the rise in the general felony crime rate, I suspect a considerable part of this is due to increased efficiency and vigilance in police departments; the more the police record crimes, the greater is the known rate. With respect to the decrease in the murder rate, the yearly differences are too small to occasion an attempted explanation here.

In most recent years in the United States, a disproportionately large number of murders have been committed during the summer months.[11] This may be due in part to a presumably greater amount of social interaction during the warm months. But, and to the best of my knowledge, no one really knows the explanation.

Further, murderers usually kill acquaintances or relatives rather than strangers. And murders are more often committed in the heat of an argument than in any other single type of situation.[12]

Relatively little research on murder has been carried out. A great deal of attention has been given to crime in the newspapers, magazines, and popular books. But few attempts have been made to understand why some people commit murder and why others do not. The research on murder that does exist is mainly of two types: psychological (including psychiatric and psychoanalytical) studies of the internal dynamics of murderers' personalities [13] and sociological studies of the social characteristics and group experiences of murderers.[14]

The late psychoanalyst, Robert Lindner, was one of the leaders of the psychological approach. Lindner seems to hold that murder is centrally an outgrowth of an unresolved Oedipus situation whereby murderers are symbolically retaliating against their parents.[15] However, he does not present evidence beyond his own analyses of several cases. There is probably some truth in his view in the sense that an unresolved Oedipus situation can be a highly frustrating experience to a child; and the frustration may have added to it many other kinds of frustration which taken together produce an aggressive, resentful individual. But to conclude that an unresolved Oedipus situation is the central factor predisposing a person toward murder seems to me gross oversimplification.

John Gillin has made the most thorough sociological study of murder.[16] He analyzed carefully the lives of ninety-six male murderers, using information gathered from records and interviews with the convicted men. He compared them with their brothers, with other types of prisoners, and with portions of the general United States population.

Gillin found that the fundamental desires of the murderers for security, ego-gratification, recognition, and new experiences were frustrated considerably. They had developed a sense of inferiority to a greater extent than their brothers. Further, the murderers were unable to compensate in socially acceptable ways for their frustrations while their brothers were much more able to do so. At the same time, the brothers were usually spared severe emotional crises which the murderers met unsuccessfully.

Most of the killings committed by the murderers in Gillin's

sample were "crimes of passion—explosive reactions to a difficult situation." [17] And ". . . more than three-fifths of the total number [of murderers] were either drunk or mentally unbalanced at the time of the crime. Most of the others were either temporarily upset emotionally or committed murder incidental to robbery or a sex crime." [18]

Gillin's is a highly valuable study and it provides definite insights into the phenomenon of murder. But a drawback of it and of other sociological studies of murderers is that the information concerning early life experience has been obtained either from incomplete written records or from the murderers. In the latter instance, the murderers could not, of course, remember anything about the first two or three years of their lives. In cases of work by psychoanalysts such as Lindner, these data about early experience have been gained from the murderer himself. Long hours of psychoanalysis, or hypnoanalysis (psychoanalysis aided by hypnosis) as Lindner sometimes used, enable the patient to verbalize about his very early years. But there is no way of knowing how much of what he remembers actually occurred as against how much of it the patient believes to have occurred.

In the study reported in this book, most of the information about the early life experience of the murderers and the control brothers was obtained from their mothers. This, of course, is by no means a perfect method. But, as will be explained, it would seem to be the best method available and the data would seem to be quite valid and reliable.

The first step in the research was to conduct a preliminary study out of which would grow the plan for the major study. Here, I tried above all to approach the phenomenon of murder with an open mind, to banish whatever preconceptions I might have about the possible influences leading to murder.

Apart from studying all the available reports of research on murder,[19] numerous biographies and autobiographies of murderers were read.[20] Probably most important, I interviewed intensively twelve convicted murderers, tried to get the feel of their personalities and the experiences which had shaped them. In

7

some cases the relatives and friends of these murderers were interviewed. In all cases I analyzed carefully the information in their prison records.

Out of all this preliminary work came one particularly striking insight: the murderers appeared to have been terribly frustrated during their early lives. By frustration I mean, fundamentally, that condition in the organism which results from lack of satisfaction of a need. The frustrations of the murderers whose lives I investigated included the following: extreme birth traumas; serious diseases in infancy and childhood; accidents of various kinds; physical beatings; severe training practices at the hands of the mother; psychological frustration due to the emotionalizing of the mother; and traumatic incidents outside the home, as well as social frustration in school and recreational situations. Of course, few murderers had experienced all of these frustrations. But a great majority had experienced many of them. And, summated, the frustration to which each had been subjected seemed much greater than that of the average person.

From this insight grew the central hypothesis for the main phase of the project: There is a significant, positive, functional relationship between the amount of frustration experienced by individuals in infancy, childhood, and adolescence, on the one hand, and whether or not they later commit murder, on the other hand. Put another way, have murderers experienced a greater amount of frustration in early life than nonmurderers? The research which followed embraced much more but this was the guiding, major "question" to be investigated.

John Dollard and his colleagues have published an especially important work on the general phenomenon of frustration titled *Frustration and Aggression*.[21] The major point Dollard and his coauthors make is presented in the form of a hypothesis: frustration always leads to aggression. Whether this is true is not known. It is simply a hypothesis. But the study of murder reported here provides one particular test of that general hypothesis since murder is a specific form of aggression.

The most general criticism concerning Dollard's frustration-aggression hypothesis [22] is that the hypothesis cannot be valid

8

because it is obvious that some people who are frustrated do not aggress against others. This is a confused criticism, however, for Dollard and his colleagues do not say that the aggression must be directed outwardly by the individual toward others; it can also be directed inwardly toward himself.

What seems to determine the direction the aggression takes is the degree of socialization of the person. The degress of socialization is the extent to which the person as a child was trained and learned to follow the accepted cultural values of his society. Thus, it is by this process that the individual develops a conscience or superego. If the individual is undersocialized, then he will presumably direct his aggression toward others in a more or less indiscriminate fashion. If he is oversocialized, he will presumably turn his aggression inwardly, upon himself; the extreme here would be suicide. Of course, there is a third possibility: reasonable, moderate socialization. Here, the individual will be likely to direct whatever aggression he has outwardly in various indirect and fairly acceptable ways.

In my preliminary research, it struck me that the murderers seemed not only to have been exposed to severe early frustration but that they also had been undersocialized. Superficially, they appeared to be quite highly socialized. As is well known, murderers generally make "good" inmates, follow prison rules well. However, in talking to the murderers about their childhood experiences I gained the impression that their parents, particularly their mothers, had in most instances been strict, highly moral people who had tried with abnormal vehemence to socialize their children. My feeling was that the parents had forced them too far and that within themselves the potential murderers had rebelled. In order tõ placate the parents, they had developed a thin crust of socialization under which there lurked a resentful, basically lawless, conscience-lacking personality.

This crust of socialization was of sufficient strength to restrain the potential murderer from committing antisocial acts in most situations, my reasoning ran. However, if they had been severely frustrated in early life, they presumably carried within them a deep reservoir of repressed aggression. That the aggressic was highly repressed seemed particularly likely since, if the frustration occurred at an early age, the potential murderers could not have had a full command of language with which to deal with it. And it is fairly certain that the less adequate is the individual's verbal ability, the more likely is repression to occur. Thus, I tentatively reasoned, when the potential murderers became involved in a particularly frustrating situation, their repressed aggression exploded out through their crustlike shell of socialization; and they killed the individual whom they conceptualized as their primary frustrater.

From the above, it should be clear that one specific, important aspect of socialization is that of aggression release. What types of channels does the individual learn to use in order to dispel his aggressive feelings? Are the channels he uses socially acceptable ones or are they socially unacceptable? How frequently does he use each channel during his childhood and adolescence?

Presumably, if he employs many acceptable channels, he will dispel his aggression without bringing down upon himself further frustration occasioned by his society's displeasure. On the other hand, if he uses unacceptable channels, it may be that he rids himself of aggressive feelings only to build up further such feelings due to frustration which results from society's unwillingness to tolerate his actions. As a third possibility, if the individual has strong feelings of aggression and seldom uses either acceptable or unacceptable channels of release, then his aggression may swell to the bursting point.

It seemed to me that murderers were likely to fall into the last two categories more frequently, proportionate to numbers, than other individuals. In testing the central hypothesis, then, it became necessary to take aggression release into account as a control factor of the first importance.

There were a number of major questions to be resolved before the field work could begin. First: What sample of murderers would be used? Second: What type of control group would be most advisable? Third: From what sources would the data be obtained? And fourth: What specific methods should be used to gather the data?

It was decided finally to select the sample of murderers from among those individuals presently serving sentences for murder or first-degree manslaughter in four New England states. Massachusetts, New Hampshire, Maine, and Rhode Island. These states were chosen largely because of financial necessity. They were nearest my home, and the cost of gathering information about murderers in those states would be considerably less than about those in other states. Most of the murderers in the four states were born and raised in New England. It is true that murderers from other regions of the United States may differ in certain respects from those in New England. However, money is a limiting factor in research as it is in most other areas of behavior in modern society.

It is also true that convicted murderers may differ from murderers who have not been apprehended. But it would be more than ridiculous to attempt inclusion of the latter in a study of murder. And convicted, imprisoned murderers may be somewhat different from convicted murderers who have been executed. Here, too, it would have been impractical to include the latter group. The main reason for the impracticality is actually not the fact that they have died but, rather, that official records on these individuals are frequently difficult or impossible to obtain.

Not all the convicted murderers in the New England states mentioned could actually be used in the sample. First, there was the question of whether to include females. After investigation of the matter, it was decided to exclude the females. They constituted such a small proportion of the total group, about 15 per cent, that it would have been impossible to handle statistically their cases in a meaningful fashion. Then there was the problem of age. It was clear that at least some of the required data would be obtained from the mothers of the murderers. Those mothers who were infirm or seriously ill would not be able to supply the information needed. Therefore, only those murderers under fifty-one years of age were included in the sample; the probability was high that mothers of men over that age could not be interviewed effectively.

Naturally, murderers who had killed their mothers or whose mothers had died by other means were also necessarily excluded. Further, those murderers whose mothers' residences were more than 150 miles from my home were not included. The cost of travel to interview the mothers would have been too great.

It was decided to use as control individuals the brothers of the murderers, which meant that only those murderers who had at least one brother could be included in the sample. Beyond that, for a murderer to be included, his control brother had to have attained, at the time of the research, at least the age the murderer was when he committed murder.

There was also the question of whether murderers who had not physically committed murder should be included. In many states, a person can be convicted of murder even though he only stood by, did not carry out the violent act himself. The decision was made to exclude these individuals from the sample. Legally, they might be murderers. But, sociologically and psychologically, it was usually the case that they were not.

Chance makes it likely that about one out of ten of the men imprisoned for murder did not actually commit the crime. As will be discussed and documented in a later chapter, 10 to 12 per cent of selected groups of individuals in the United States who have been executed or imprisoned for life in recent years have later been found to be innocent. In the case of my research, there was no way of determining which convicted individuals were innocent. Nonetheless, the likelihood that a few of the "murderers" are not guilty should be borne in mind.

The sample of murderers, then, was composed of individuals who met the following criteria: (1) convicted of murder or first-degree manslaughter; (2) serving sentence during the period November 1, 1957, to February 8, 1958; (3) imprisoned in Massachusetts, New Hampshire, Maine, or Rhode Island; (4) male; (5) under fifty-one years of age; (6) mother living; (7) mother able to answer questions in English; (8) mother residing within 150 miles of Durham, New Hampshire; (9) at least one brother who had attained the age the murderer was when he committed murder; and (10) the court records must have indicated that the individual was believed to have physically committed the murder.

There were 254 male individuals in the four states who were serving sentences for murder or first-degree manslaughter. Of these, seventy-six met all the above criteria. The sample later decreased to fifty-one subjects because nineteen mothers were not available for a variety of reasons and six mothers refused to be interviewed. The mothers were, in general, much more willing to grant interviews than I had anticipated.

After considering the various possibilities, I decided to use the brothers of the murderers as the control subjects. They were, in many ways, ideal. They possessed similar heredity, had usually been brought up in the same home and neighborhood as the murderers. Further, their race, nationality, preadult religion, and pre-adult social class positions were equivalent to those of the murderers. But they had not committed murder. Why was it the one brother had killed and the other had not?

A major drawback of the use of brothers as control subjects was the fact that murderers who were only-children would be excluded from the sample. And it is possible, although far from certain, that only-children differ in certain important respects from other individuals. However, this one outstanding liability was far outweighed by the previously mentioned assets of the approach used.

There was the question of which brother to choose as a control subject when the murderer had more than one brother. It was logical to choose that brother who was nearest in age to the murderer—providing the brother had, at the time of the research, lived at least as many years as had the murderer when he killed. Obviously, an additional criterion had to be employed here: the brother could not have been convicted of murder or first-degree manslaughter. Of interest is the fact that none of the potential control brothers had been so convicted. And few of them, only about 12 per cent, had reformatory, jail, or prison records.

These were, then, the two groups of subjects: fifty-one men who had each been legally convicted of killing one or more of his fellow human beings; and an equal number of men, their brothers, who to the best of anyone's knowledge had never murdered.

The next major question to be resolved was this: from what sources would the data be obtained? What were the most valid and practical sources? Clearly, prison or department of correction records would be the best source for data about the general characteristics of the murderers and about the nature of the crimes. But there were several alternatives to the question of the source or sources from which to gather information about the frustration experiences and aggression release patterns of the murderers and their brothers. In the cases of the murderers some of this information would be in prison records. But it would not be uniform and there would not, of course, be any such information about the murderers' brothers. Therefore, for these data about frustration and aggression release prison records were an inadequate source.

Would the murderers and brothers themselves be a fruitful source for these data? They might be for information about their experiences after the ages of four or five. But they would have little or no knowledge of the first few years of their lives—in many ways the crucial years. Their parents seemed, in the final analysis, the only adequate source of information about frustration and socialization. And of the two parents, the mother would know a great deal more about these factors than the father. This is not to say that the fathers were necessarily less important influences than the mothers in the development of the murderers and their brothers. But the fathers generally would not know nearly as much about the particulars of the early lives of their children as would the mothers.

What methods should be used to obtain the data? In the case of data to be gathered from the prison records, a schedule completed by me or some other researcher working on the project would be best. We would read through each murderer's file at the department of correction or prison and fill in on the schedule the information needed.

In the case of data to be obtained from the mothers, two possibilities existed: one, send the mothers questionnaires and ask them to complete them; two, interview the mothers using a schedule of definite questions. The first possibility was a poor one because many mothers would not have the motivation to complete the questionnaires; others with little education or low intelligence would not be able to answer the questions even if they were motivated to do so. The second possibility, interviewing the mothers, was the only feasible one. Because the mothers were located in many cities and towns in four states, this would be a time-consuming, costly task. But it was the only way to obtain the information needed.

Once these questions were resolved, the field work began. The first step was to gain the co-operation of the commissioners of correction and the prison wardens in the four New England states. I wrote these men letters explaining the project and requesting interviews with them. All agreed to talk with me about the study on which I had embarked. I found that each of these men welcomed the idea of my project.

An assistant, a graduate student in sociology, and I checked the files of the 254 male murderers and first-degree manslaughterers imprisoned in the four states. Those cases which did not fit the criteria previously mentioned were quickly weeded out. The files of the seventy-six remaining men were carefully studied. Data were extracted from those files in order that the forty-two questions on the information schedules could be answered. These questions ranged from name and address of mother to method by which the murder was committed to intelligence quotient of the murderer.

Next, the schedule for interviewing the mothers was constructed. This schedule was thirty-two pages in length and contained 143 questions. Most of the questions were of the closed-ended type; that is, there were several possible answers, one of which could be checked by the interviewer. These interview questions were carefully constructed, revised; some were eliminated, new ones added. Then came a test of the schedule. First, it was, for convenience sake, tested on a few arbitrarily chosen mothers who had not reared murderers. Here a number of poorly phrased questions were changed. Then the schedule was tested on several mothers of murderers. Again the schedule was revised. Finally, it was in the proper form.

The interviewing of the seventy-six mothers of the murderers and control brothers began. This, together with the twelve interviews of murderers I had done in the preliminary phase of the study, was the most interesting aspect of the whole venture. One could "see" the mothers' personalities in operation. As the mothers answered the questions dealing with the early life experiences of the murderers, one seemed to sense the onset of catastrophe, the almost inevitable development toward the crime of murder.

The interviews were carried out by me and by two men who had considerable experience in interviewing. Above all, the interviewers were chosen for their ability to relate to others understandingly and warmly. It was, in this case, particularly necessary to have interviewers who had the capacity to make those being interviewed feel at ease, not inferior or defensive.

The mothers lived in cities and towns from Rhode Island to Maine. Hence, a great deal of traveling was required. The mothers were seldom telephoned or written before the interviewer went to the residence. I was convinced that prior notification of the interview would lead many of the mothers to avoid it in one way or another. So, the usual procedure was to meet the mother without giving her any "warning."

Before going to the mother's home, I or whoever was to conduct the interview would familiarize himself with the information about the case which had been obtained from official files. It was of course necessary to know the first names of the murderer and his brother, to know the particulars of the murder, and so on. A few of the murderers had killed members of their families; obviously, it was important to know something such as this before approaching the mother.

The mother would come to the door, open it slightly, and frequently say, "Yes?" in what struck me as a semisuspicious fashion. I would explain that I was a sociologist or researcher and that "we are doing a study of why boys get in trouble with the law." The word murder was never mentioned during the interview. I would then say to the mother, "Would you be willing to talk to me for a while about your son?"

Generally, the mother would say, "All right. Come in." There was not as much resistance here as one might expect. My feeling is that the mothers tended unconsciously to sense that the interview would provide a catharsis; most mothers appeared to have some guilt feelings about their sons' crimes. Further, I think that in some instances the mothers welcomed a brief return to the limelight. That is to say, many had been in the public eye during and shortly after the trial. They had received attention, however negative it may have been. But this had faded and now some of the mothers had, I believe, an at least unconscious desire to regain a place, any kind of place, in the social sun.

We would sit down and I would explain that I wanted to ask about her sons' early lives in some detail. "It will take an hour or two," I would say. "But I can promise that this will not hurt your sons in any way. What we are trying to do is to find out all we can about why boys get in certain kinds of trouble with the law so that we can help boys in general from getting in trouble." I would then explain why I wanted to gain information about the son who was the control brother as well as about the one who was imprisoned. Usually the mothers seemed to understand all this, find it reasonable.

Only one child was dealt with at a time. When all the questions were asked about one son, we turned to the other son. The schedule was designed so that the same questions were asked about the murderer as about his brother. In other words, when interviewing a mother, two copies of the schedule were completed: one for each of the two sons. In the cases of a few questions, such as number of children in the family, the mother was not asked twice, of course. But the answers to the great majority of the questions were likely to be different for one child than the other.

The attempt was made to alternate the order in which the lives of the two children were investigated. In interviewing one mother, the questions were asked first about the murderer and then about the control brother. With the next mother, the sequence was reversed, if feasible. There were instances where this was not practical. Some mothers could not understand, at the beginning, the necessity for asking questions about the son who had "never been in trouble." Later in the interview, however, these mothers were willing to answer the questions about that son. In any case, the order of questioning was alternated to the extent possible. This was done to allow for differences in the mother's answers that might be due to her familiarity with the questions when they were asked a second time or to fatigue during the latter part of the interview.

Actually, the interviews did not take as long as one might think. They lasted from one hour and fifteen minutes to three hours, with the average being nearer the shorter time. This was possible because many of the questions were designed in such a way that they could be very readily answered. Then, too, some of the questions did not apply in a given case and could be skipped.

The mothers were usually exceedingly able to remember the details of the early lives of their children. For most women, the bringing-up of their children is the most important set of events in their lives. And they can frequently remember those events with much more clarity than they can remember more recent events of a different nature. Some of the questions on the interview schedule were designed to elicit information that had already been obtained from the prison records. This was done in order to provide a check on the mothers' memories and truthfulness. The answers given by the mothers corresponded very closely to the information in the records.

For example, in the cases of thirty-three murderers, data concerning illnesses and accidents which occurred during their early lives were extracted from the prison files. These data had not been supplied originally by the mothers. Eighty-eight per cent of the illnesses and accidents were accurately reported by the mothers, using the data from the files as the criterion.

Of course, there is the possibility that the mothers might have distorted the truth with respect to factors that could not be checked against the prison records, such as the ways they trained their children in infancy and early childhood. There is no way of knowing to what extent this occurred. My feeling is that the mothers' answers reflected what actually happened quite accurately. I do not think the mothers had reason to lie and I do not think their memories were distorted to any significant degree.

The mothers were never told during the interview of any possible types of relationship between their answers and whether their sons became murderers. It would require a person with some knowledge of sociology and psychology to perceive any connection between, let us say, early frustration and murder. None of the mothers appeared to possess that knowledge. And it would be this type of perception that would lead to lying.

With respect to the mothers' memories being in error, the probability seems low. I have purposely questioned some mothers who did not rear murderers about the early lives of their children. In these cases it was possible to check their statements. The mothers' memories were substantially correct.

Therefore, I feel the probability is high that the responses of the murderers' mothers represented quite accurately the actual situations. But the possibility of distortion cannot be ruled out completely.

As the interviews drew to a close, the mothers frequently seemed reluctant to have me leave. They had grown tired of answering questions and they had "talked themselves out." Yet they wanted me to stay. It was as if they now wanted to ask a question but did not know how to phrase it. It was as if they wanted a definite answer to an unformulated question. I think the question they could not formulate was, "Why, why did he do it?" And had they been able to ask the question, I could not have answered it. Had I known the answer, there would have been no need for me to make the study.

To determine whether the differences between the murderer and control brother groups were statistically significant, the chi-square (X^2) test was used. Those readers not familiar with this test may find the following explanation helpful: If immediately after the chi-square number, $X^2 = 15.012$ for example, there appears the designation, $P < 0.01$, this means that the observed differences between murderer and brother groups can be attributed to chance less than 1 per cent of the time. This is usually accepted as a statistically significant relationship.

Following some chi-square numbers will be found the designation, $P < 0.05$. Here, the observed differences between the murderer and brother groups can be attributed to chance five times or less out of one hundred times. This, though to a lesser extent than in the first test, is accepted as a statistically significant relationship. On the other hand, the designation, $P > 0.05$, indicates that the probability of a chance relationship is greater than five out of one hundred and the functional relationship is not considered statistically significant.

Many nonresearchers resent the use of even simple statistics when one is dealing with human behavior, murderous or otherwise. There is a feeling that there is something both impossible and vaguely immoral about analyzing behavior in this way. This is nonsense. If we are ever to understand the influences behind behavior, we shall have to rely on statistical tools for transposing those influences and that behavior into forms that lend themselves to scientific generalizations. To rely solely on armchair analyses, as so many nonresearchers wish to do, will get us nowhere. At the same time, the researcher should not ignore the individual cases, the particular human being. He should attempt to illustrate his statistical findings with the living stuff of human experience.

In this chapter, then, the general background of the study, the problems encountered, and the procedures used have been explained in some detail. Therefore, it is now possible to present the results, the actual findings, of the study.

2. *The Murderers and the Murders*

VARIOUS CHARACTERISTICS of the murderers, their families, the murders, and the victims will be summarized in this chapter. In the chapters which follow, data which bear more directly on the central hypothesis of the study will be presented.

There were no professional killers among the fifty-one murderers studied. Contrary to a fairly widespread belief, most murders are committed by individuals who may best be called nonprofessionals.[1] Four of the fifty-one men in the group had been convicted of murder or first-degree manslaughter prior to their present conviction. However, these four cases could in no way be classified as of the murder-for-hire type.

On the other hand, twenty-three of the murderers had been convicted of a felony other than murder or first-degree manslaughter at some time previous to the beginning of their present imprisonment. Only thirteen of these men had actually served time in prison for their crimes. The other ten had been placed on probation, indicating that their crimes were not of the most serious types. One of the murderers did have a record of thirty-two convictions and had served several prison terms. He was an alcoholic who frequently violated the law when intoxicated. But the majority of the fifty-one men had either minor or no conviction records.

Two of the murderers had each committed two almost simultaneous killings for which they were imprisoned at the time of this study. One of these men, a deaf mute, clubbed his wife and infant daughter to death in a fit of rage. The other, an unmarried man of twenty-seven, killed a girl who was apparently a prostitute and her aged mother. The remaining forty-nine men were not imprisoned for multiple murders.

On the basis of the information available, only a small minority of the fifty-three murders, seven in number, can be said to have been consciously planned. Most of these seven were not carefully planned. Typical here is the murder committed by a husband whose wife was having dates with another man. The husband saw his wife in a café with the other man. He got in his car, drove seven miles to his home, picked up a gun. He then returned to the café and shot his wife's lover. He had made no plans for escape and was easily apprehended.

Of the remaining forty-six murders, twenty were committed in what can best be called "the heat of argument." The potential murderer would build up aggression during an argument with a stranger, a slight acquaintance, his wife, or other relative, then suddenly kill with either his bare hands or a club of some sort.

Nineteen of the murders were committed in connection with another crime, but the murders themselves could not be said to have been consciously planned. And the other crimes were rarely of the professional burglary or holdup type. Usually they were either rape cases or amateurish holdups where the victims resisted. The circumstances surrounding the remaining seven cases could not be accurately determined.

With respect to the murders which occurred in conjunction with other crimes, the example of two young boys, fifteen and sixteen years old, comes to mind. Both were from lower-class families where the parents clearly rejected them. The boys attempted to hold up an old man. He fought back and they beat him to death with a broken bottle and a heavy stick. The boys were convicted and sent directly to a state prison, not a reformatory. One was sentenced for life, the other for ten to thirty-three years. The mother of the boy sentenced for life—not at all typical of the mothers, incidentally—said, "If that's the kind of thing he's going to do, he can rot in prison as far as I'm concerned." She was a large, sullen, openly aggressive woman. "Me go to see him?"

she said. "The hell with him. He was always causing me trouble, ever since he could walk, if you know what I mean."

Shooting was the most prevalent method used to kill by the murderers studied. Seventeen of the fifty-three murders were committed by this means. Knifing, on the other hand, accounted for only seven of the murders. It is of interest to note that it is commonly found that male murderers tend to use firearms while females tend to use knives. Possibly this is because males are more familiar with firearms and have easier access to them; females have familiarity with kitchen knives. The total distribution of methods used by the fifty-one murderers in committing the fifty-three murders is shown in Table 1. There were no cases of poisoning in spite of what detective stories might lead one to think.

Table 1
*Methods Used to Commit the Murders ***

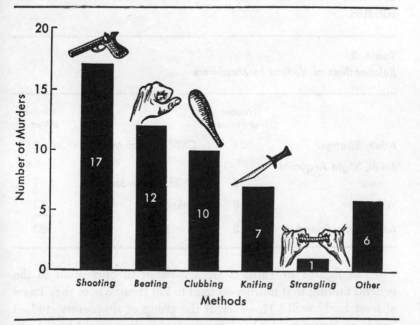

* Total number of cases = 53.

Using police records and excerpts of court trials as the sources, it was found that only one of the fifty-one men was highly intoxicated at the time of his crime. Thirteen had definitely been drinking but were moderately intoxicated at most. Nineteen were known to have been completely sober. In the cases of the remaining eighteen men, their states of intoxication, if any, were unknown. But it is likely that if these eighteen murderers had been highly intoxicated, this information would have been included in the police and court records.

Therefore, we can say that consumption of alcohol was not, in the cases studied here, strikingly associated with the crimes. My own feeling is that the use of alcohol does not have much bearing on whether an individual commits murder. I suspect that if he is motivated to kill, he will do so, regardless of whether or not he drinks.

The sexes of the victims were almost evenly divided: twenty-seven males and twenty-six females. Table 2 indicates the ways in which the victims' relationships to the murderers were distributed.

Table 2
Relationships of Victims to Murderers

	Number of Victims		Number of Victims
Adult, Stranger	21	Child, Not of Murderer	2
Adult, Slight Acquaintance	15	Child, of Murderer	1
Wife	8	Unknown	3
Adult, Close Friend	3	Total	53

The figures in Table 2 are somewhat in opposition to the general finding that murderers tend to kill those whom they know at least fairly well.[2] However, if the group of murderers studied had been larger in number, that general finding might have been borne out. In any event, those murderers included in my research killed strangers in 39 per cent of the cases and slight acquaintances in 28 per cent.

Here is a somewhat startling finding: of those murderers in the group who were married at the time they killed, a majority killed their wives. Only fifteen of the fifty-one men were married at that time and, as shown in Table 2, eight took their wives' lives. In the cases of five of these eight murderers, their mothers said they believed that their sons' relationships with their wives had been disharmonious in the months preceding the murders.

The ages of the murderers at the times they committed the murders varied considerably. The mean age was twenty-three years while the oldest murderer was thirty-five and the youngest fifteen. (None could have been fifty-one or over because of the nature of choosing the sample.) Thirteen of the fifty-one men were under twenty when they killed, and all of these had been sent directly to a state prison upon being sentenced. Many states do not have special facilities for caring for juveniles who have committed violent crimes.

Forty-one of the murderer group had been convicted of murder rather than manslaughter. Of these forty-one men, a large majority were convicted of first-degree murder. The remaining ten in the group had been found guilty of first-degree manslaughter or its equivalent.

Thirty-five men were sentenced to life imprisonment and sixteen to terms ranging from eight to sixty years. At the time of this research, the fifty-one murderers had, on the average, served seven years of their sentences.

According to the departments of correction files, prison psychiatrists and psychologists judged that, as of the end of 1957, thirteen of the fifty-one murderers were quite normal emotionally; thirteen were stated to have severe neurotic symptoms; four were diagnosed as psychotic; ten were classified as psychopathic personalities; and in the cases of the remaining eleven, there was no psychological report in the files.

It will be remembered that if a murderer's mother did not live within 150 miles of Durham, New Hampshire, he was excluded from the study. Therefore, few conclusions can be drawn from a distribution of the states in which the murderers were imprisoned. However, for the reader's interest, this distribution by state was: thirty-eight in Massachusetts; six in New Hampshire; four in Maine; and three in Rhode Island.

The mothers were not, as a group, unusually young or old at the times of the murderers' births. Five mothers were under twenty years of age, thirty-three were between twenty and twenty-nine, and thirteen were in their thirties. None was forty or older.

The mothers were asked the question: "Was the child's father or stepfather living in the home during a majority of the first six years of the child's life?" In the cases of the murderers, forty-seven mothers said the child's father was living in the home, one mother said a stepfather was living in the home, and the remaining three mothers said neither father nor stepfather was. In the cases of the control brothers, the picture was much the same: forty-six mothers answered that the child's father was living in the home, one said a stepfather was, and four said neither was.

There is indicated, then, an amazingly low rate of physical separation of the parents during the early years of life of the children. In almost all cases there was a father-figure in the home during the formative years of the child. Often, it appeared that the father was a passive man given to occasional outbursts of aggression. But, in any case, he was a part of the family. My feeling is that the parents of murderers tend to be people who conform rigidly to certain, although by no means all, moral codes. One of the codes to which they seem to conform is that married couples will not separate or divorce. They may not get on well, one or both of them may drink heavily, but they stick together.

This was well illustrated in my interview with the mother of Robert McAllister, a young man who had killed during a decidedly amateurish holdup. A small man in his fifties answered the door. It was midafternoon and he was clearly intoxicated. "No, she's in the apartment across the hall," he said, and closed the door without undue conversation.

I found Mrs. McAllister across the hall baby-sitting for her daughter. The small man was her husband and she said to me,

"I can't stand him. I never could. I spend most of my time over here, sitting for Rose."

"Why can't you stand him?"

Mrs. McAllister was fifty years of age but appeared fifteen or twenty years older; several of her front teeth were missing. She was poor and always had been. She had completed only five years of school. But she could express herself well and I would estimate her over-all I.Q. to be about 110.

"I can't stand him because he drinks and gets mean as a bull," she said. "He always has. He's all right when he's sober but he never is."

"This was true when Robert was a little boy?"

"Before that. Ever since I met him. Why I married him I don't know."

"But you've been married over thirty years. Why was it you never separated or divorced?"

Mrs. McAllister shrugged her shoulders and gave a mild snort. "I don't know. When I married, I married for life, I suppose. We weren't brought up like some people, divorcing all the time."

Later she said, "Oh, it was hard during the first years. Why, when I married him he had a case of the—you know—the venereal disease. I've got the papers to prove it." She showed me an old letter stating such and signed by a doctor of medicine. She carried the letter in her handbag.

"It was hard at first, him drinking all the time, beating up me and the kids. But after a while I just decided I'd keep out of his way as much as I could and I did."

"Did he beat one of the children more than the rest?" There had been thirteen children in the family.

"Bobby he beat the most." Bobby was the murderer. "Bobby was the oldest and he never liked him."

According to Mrs. McAllister, Robert developed a phobia with respect to his father and from the ages of two to fifteen was terrified of him, especially at ages five and six. Contrary to popular belief, a home broken by separation or divorce sometimes has a less negative effect on a child's development than the opposite.

A considerable majority of the mothers did not work outside the home to any prolonged extent when their children were young. During the period when the murderers were born until they were six years of age, thirty-nine of the fifty-one mothers did not work outside the home for a total time of six months or more. During a like period in the lives of the control brothers, forty-one of the mothers did not work for more than six months.

Superficially, the early home lives of the murderers and their brothers appear to have been quite adequate for normal development. The murderers' parents seem to have been looked upon by members of the community as poor but generally respectable, conscientious individuals. (I make this statement on the basis of conversations I had with people who had been neighbors of the parents when the murderers and brothers were children.) However, beneath the surface the parents presented to the outside world, there seems to have existed a disorganization of family relationships that could readily contribute to a growing pattern of maladjustment in the developing child. Future chapters will partially document this statement.

One of the murderers was the fraternal twin of his control brother; the others were not twins of the controls. The number of children born into the families, including the murderers and the control brothers, ranged from two to fourteen. The average number was 5.2. Fourteen murderers and nineteen brothers were the oldest children in their families while fifteen murderers and nine brothers were youngest children. Because of the fact that the control brothers had to have attained the age the murderers were when they committed murder, nothing conclusive can be drawn from these sibling-rank figures. Still, it is of interest to note that of the twenty-four murderers and brothers who were youngest children in their families, the murderers accounted for 62.5 per cent; while of those thirty-three who were oldest children, the murderers constituted only 42.4 per cent.

With respect to race, forty-six of the murderers and forty-six of the control brothers were white and five of each were Negro. About 10 per cent of the murderers, then, were Negro. But in 1950 Negroes constituted only 1.5 per cent of the population of the six New England states.[3] Of course, the fifty-one murderers were imprisoned in only four of those states. Further, not all of the fifty-one had grown up in New England. Nevertheless, Negroes were six to seven times more prevalent in the group studied than were Negroes in the general New England population during the "average year" in which the murders were committed. This approximates the previously mentioned statistics which indicate a rate of murder conviction for Negroes that is much higher than for whites.

The differences in rates by race may be due in part to prejudice which leads Negroes to be arrested for murder more often than whites. Also, because of prejudice, Negroes have at their disposal less means—political influence and money to hire efficient lawyers—for escaping conviction once arrested. Still further, the social frustration experienced by Negroes due to prejudice may contribute to a build-up of aggressive feelings which sometimes result in murder.

Table 3 shows the nationality backgrounds of the parents of the murderers. They were predominantly English, Scottish, north Irish, south Irish, and French.

Table 3
*Nationality Backgrounds of Parents of Murderers ***

	Number of Mothers	Number of Fathers		Number of Mothers	Number of Fathers
English, Scottish, North Irish	11	14	Portuguese	1	1
South Irish	10	9	Polish	0	1
French	8	7	German	1	0
Yankee **	5	5	Swedish	1	0
Italian	4	4	Other	7	6
Greek	2	2	Unknown	0	1
Russian	1	1	Total	51	51

* Determined by male ancestry.
** Five mothers insisted they and their husbands were Yankee and would state no foreign nationality background.

29

A more striking factor than nationality background is that of the religion of the murderers. The mothers were asked what were the religious preferences of the murderers at age eighteen. Thirty-four of the murderers were said to have been Roman Catholics, twelve to have been Protestants, and one to have been a Jew. Two were reported to have been of other religious faiths and one to have had no religion. In the remaining two cases the mothers simply did not know.

Table 4

Extent to Which Mothers Said They Liked Neighbors during First 6 Years of Life of Murderers and Control Brothers

	Number of Mothers	
	During Murderers' First 6 Years	During Brothers' First 6 Years
Very Much	24	25
Moderately	12	13
Very Little	13	11
Not at All	1	1
Doesn't Apply *	1	1
Total	51	51

* No neighbors.

Forty of the murderers spent majorities of the first six years of their lives in cities of five thousand or more population. Five spent those years in cities or towns with less than five thousand population. And the remaining six lived in the open country. The figures for the murderers' brothers were about the same. Thirty-four of the murderers and thirty-four of their brothers spent majorities of their first six years of life in poor neighborhoods of low prestige. Sixteen in each group spent the same years in neighborhoods of average prestige. And only one in each group lived in a residential area of high prestige.[4]

The mothers were asked how well they liked the people in

the neighborhood where they had lived during the first six years of life of the murderers and the brothers. If they had lived in more than one neighborhood, they were asked the question about the neighborhood where they had lived for the longest period during the six years. By and large the mothers seemed to like the people around them fairly well, as Table 4 shows.

I had thought that the mothers might have disliked those living near them to a considerable extent, especially when the murderers were young. But this does not appear to have been the case. As will be seen in later chapters, frequently the mothers were definitely maladjusted in certain respects. However, as I got to know them through the interviews, it became clear that they had been and were women who generally succeeded in getting along with the people around them—other than the members of their own families.

With respect to educational level attained, none of the fifty-one murderers had attended college and only three had graduated from high school. Seventeen had attended high school but had not graduated. Six had completed the eighth grade and then stopped their education. Twenty-three had completed one to seven years of school only. (Data were not available for the two remaining cases.)

Thus, a majority of the fifty-one men did not go beyond the eighth grade. One can roughly compare this with the median number of years of school completed by males twenty-five years of age or older who were living in the New England states in 1950. This figure was 10.1 years.[5] However, the murderers' relative lack of educational attainment was not due to stupidity. Table 5 presents the over-all intelligence quotients of the murderers.

Of the thirty-seven murderers whose over-all I.Q.'s were known, a slight majority, nineteen, had I.Q.'s of 100 or more, 100 being the average for the general United States population. Most of these men were tested just after they had been committed to a state prison. I suspect that in many cases the confusion and resentment of the convicted men made their scores lower than they would have been under more normal circumstances. As for the fourteen unknown cases, there is no reason to think that their

I.Q.'s were markedly low. Those individuals of especially low intelligence who commit murder are usually sent to mental hospitals rather than prisons.

The facts that none of the murderers was known to have an I.Q. of 140 or higher and that none had gone to college should not lead one to conclude that extremely intelligent people and college graduates do not commit murder. Near the end of this

Table 5
Over-All Intelligence Quotients of Murderers *

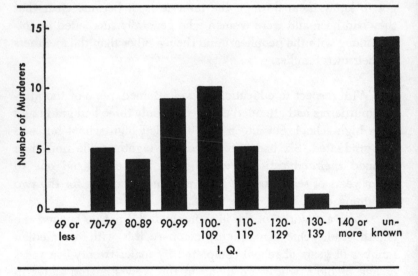

* Total number of cases = 51.

book, I shall present the case of a man, not one of the fifty-one men in the sample, who is a college graduate and who has an I.Q. of over 140.

The educational levels attained by the parents of the murderers were in general rather low. Only three of the fathers and none of the mothers graduated from college. Three fathers and four mothers graduated from high school but not from college. Forty-three fathers and forty-seven mothers completed the eighth grade but did not complete high school. (The mothers did not know the educational levels of the remaining two fathers.)

The occupational prestige of the fathers, at the times when the murderers were born, tended also to be low. Hollingshead's seven-point scale of occupational prestige [6] is used here to classify the fathers with respect to this factor. As can be seen in Table 6, only six of the fathers had occupations in the three highest prestige categories. But a substantial majority of the fathers, thirty-seven in number, had occupations which fell into the lowest two categories of prestige.

Table 6
Occupational Prestige of Fathers When Murderers Were Born

	Number of Fathers
I Higher Executives, Proprietors of Large Concerns, Major Professionals	1
II Business Managers, Proprietors of Medium Businesses, Lesser Professionals	2
III Administrative Personnel, Owners of Small Businesses, Semiprofessionals	3
IV Clerical and Sales Workers, Technicians, Owners of Very Small Businesses	0
V Skilled Manual Employees	8
VI Semiskilled Employees	19
VII Unskilled Employees	18
Total	51

As for the murderers themselves, their occupational prestige levels just before they committed murder were in general very low. Slightly over half were unskilled employees while only one had an occupation that was classifiable in any of the three highest prestige categories.

Hollingshead has also developed a Two-Factor Index of Social Position,[7] i.e., of social class standing. This index takes into consideration the above-mentioned factors of educational level attained and occupational prestige. Using the index, the fathers can be classified with respect to social class as of the times when the murderers were born. Class I is, of course, that of highest prestige, and Class V is that of lowest prestige. Only one father was in Class I. Two fathers were in Class II and two in Class III. Seventeen were in Class IV and a majority, twenty-seven, were in Class V. (The class position could not be calculated for two fathers.)

There is no way of knowing the social class distributions of the communities into which the murderers were born. However, Hollingshead did class-stratify the population of a New England city, New Haven, Connecticut, as of 1950.[8] And in the late 1930's, Warner stratified the population of Newburyport, Massachusetts.[9] Warner found six social classes in that city. However, his classes I and II correspond approximately to Class I as determined by Hollingshead's Index of Social Position. Thus, a very rough comparison can be made between the social class distributions of the fathers of the murderers and of the residents of New Haven and Newburyport.

The fathers of the murderers tended to be concentrated in the lowest class, Class V, much more than did the residents of New Haven or Newburyport. Over half of the fathers were in Class V while less than a fifth of New Haveners and about a quarter of Newburyport residents were in that class. Only about one-tenth of the fathers were in classes I, II, and III; but over three-tenths of New Haveners and over four-tenths of Newburyport residents were in those three highest classes. (See Table 1, Appendix A, for details.)

While these comparisons with the New Haven and Newburyport populations are far from refined, it is fairly clear that the murderers studied were born into families of the lowest social class much more often than are New Englanders in general. I think part of the explanation is that children who grow up in Class V families experience greater frustration than those children who develop in higher social class families.

The mothers were asked what types of boys the murderers and their brothers associated with recreationally when they were about sixteen years old. Quite clearly, according to the mothers, more of the murderers than of the brothers associated with delinquents. Fourteen of the murderers and only two of the brothers were said to have associated predominantly with boys whom the mothers defined as delinquent. On the other hand, thirty of the murderers and practically all of the brothers, forty-eight in number, were reported to have associated predominantly with non-delinquents. (The mothers did not know in the cases of seven murderers and one brother.) When tested by chi-square these differences are statistically significant as is shown in Table 2 of Appendix A.

Also, the mothers were asked the extent to which the murderers and their brothers dated girls at about age seventeen. They said that only four of the murderers dated once a week or more while sixteen of the brothers did so. And, reported the mothers, fifteen of the murderers never dated when about age seventeen while this was true for but nine brothers. These are significant differences. (See Table 3, Appendix A.)

Only seventeen, or one-third, of the murderers had been married. On the other hand, thirty-three of the control brothers, or about two-thirds, had married by the time of this study. Of course, some of the murderers who might have married were prohibited from doing so by imprisonment. But imprisonment probably doesn't account fully for the large discrepancy. In my judgment, anxiety about heterosexual matters was a factor which kept a relatively large proportion of the murderers from marrying.

According to the mothers, the control brothers' relationships with their wives were harmonious in a significantly greater proportion of instances than was the case with the murderers. The mothers believed that twenty-six of the thirty-three married control brothers generally had harmonious relationships with their wives. This was true for only seven of the seventeen married murderers. Conversely, four of the thirty-three brothers were said to have had generally disharmonious relationships while ten of the seventeen murderers were placed in this category by the mothers.

The latter did not know in the cases of three brothers. (See Table 4, Appendix A, for the chi-square figure.)

The experience of psychological therapy was considered a potential control variable of significance. However, only four of the fifty-one murderers received therapy before the murders. And only three of the control brothers were exposed to therapy. Therefore, it was, in the final analysis, not necessary to treat therapy as a control factor when analyzing frustration-aggression differences between the two groups.

True, if the murderers had received efficient therapy before they committed murder, a number of them might never have come to the point of carrying out the crime. But that is a matter that will be discussed in the concluding chapter.

The material presented in this chapter can be summarized by presenting a brief picture of the hypothetically typical murderer of the group of fifty-one men studied. He was twenty-three years old when he committed murder. He had previously been convicted of some crime but had not been imprisoned. Using a firearm, and in the heat of argument, he killed a male who was a stranger to him. He had not been drinking heavily at the time. He was convicted of first-degree murder and sentenced to life imprisonment in the state of Massachusetts. At the time of this research he had served seven years of his sentence. He manifested definite neurotic, psychotic, or psychopathic personality symptoms.

The typical murderer was white, Catholic, and neither the oldest nor the youngest child in the family. During his infancy and childhood, his parents were living together. His mother did not work outside the home. He grew up in a low-prestige residential area of a New England community of over five thousand population.

Of average intelligence, he attended a public school but broke off his education before entering high school, as had both of his parents. His father was a semiskilled worker. The family was in the lowest social class in the community. He himself worked intermittently in an unskilled capacity. He had dated girls only infrequently as an adolescent and had never married.

From the material presented in this chapter, then, there are the beginnings of a picture of the fifty-one murderers as individuals who by and large had led dismal, unprestigeful, frustrating lives. Further chapters will fill out this picture in detail.

The Case of James La Casse

JAMES LA CASSE is not typical of the twelve murderers interviewed in the preliminary phase of this study; neither is he typical of the fifty-one murderers in the main phase of the study. No one of these individuals can be considered fully representative of either group. As will be seen, they do have certain important characteristics in common. Still, each is an individual in his own right. However, the case of James La Casse is one which will serve well as a further introduction to the world in which the murderer develops and to the world which he perceives as an adult.

I interviewed James La Casse for three and one-half hours. Following that, I interviewed his mother and father separately and at length. I talked with police officials who had worked on the case and with two young men who had known La Casse before the crime.

The interview with James La Casse took place in a small private room in the prison. A guard led La Casse into the room and immediately left, closing the door behind him. I held out my hand and La Casse took it. I explained who I was and indicated that he should sit down across the table from me.

James La Casse looked like an uncertain, good-natured fifteen-year-old. Actually he was twenty and he had the year before murdered a four-year-old girl.

I knew that La Casse worked in the prison woodworking shop and so I said to him, "How do you like your work here in the prison?"

"Oh, it's all right. But you can't learn a trade out of it, you know?"

"Why is that?"

"Well, they just don't teach you, you know? I mean you cut boards up and like that but, well, you can't learn a trade out of it."

There were three striking things about James La Casse. The first was that he seldom looked at you. He looked down and to his left as he spoke, occasionally glancing up as if to be sure you were still there. The second was that he continually rubbed his hands as if washing them. The third was less tangible, an attitude which implied that he was perpetually waiting for something to happen.

"How are you getting along in prison?" I asked him. "Do you have a good record here?"

"Pretty good, you know?" Always that questioning "you know" at the end of a phrase. "Pretty good except for in solitary. I didn't like that so hot." He glanced at me, then back down at the floor, and went on. "You didn't know about that?"

"No."

"I was in for four days. This fellow in the next cell to me, he wanted to make a break, you know? Get out? He wanted me to get him some nails, big ones—no, spikes they were, from the shop. Where I work? I got them for him. He wanted me to break out with him. But I wouldn't. But I got him the nails—the spikes. They found them on me so he got twelve days in solitary and I got four—because I didn't really want to break out?"

"It was pretty hard on you in solitary?"

"Well, they give you some things. Regular meals. But no cigarettes. Nobody to talk to. Nothing to read. A light burning, all the time?" Now his hands washed each other continuously, symbolically. "The worst thing was, it was dirty in there, you know? There wasn't nothing to clean it up with. I asked them for a rag, something to clean it up with. At first they wouldn't give it to me but then they did and in a day I had that cell cleaned up spotless. I wet the rag in the toilet bowl, you know?"

"And then you felt better?"

"Well, yeah. I like things nice. Clean." He shook his head without looking at me. "I like things clean. Everything——"

"Suppose they kept you in a cell for a long time and wouldn't let you clean it?"

"Wouldn't what?"

"Wouldn't let you clean it up."

"I don't know. I'd get nervous, you know? But I'd ask them for a rag."

"Suppose they wouldn't give it to you. What would you do?"

He shrugged his shoulders, not looking at me. "I'd scream. I'd scream until they gave me something to clean it up with."

We talked further and then I said to him, "Tell me about the situation when you killed the four-year-old girl?"

He laughed slightly, nervously. "Kathy, you mean?"

"Yes."

"Well, it was——" He stopped and there was just the moving of his hands over each other.

"How did you get to know her?" I asked him.

"Well, it was—she moved into the house across the street. Two weeks before, you know? Her family and mine, they got to know each other. They'd come over to the house and they'd bring her, Kathy? Or sometimes my family would go over there and Kathy would come over and stay with me. We liked each other, you know? I used to take her down the block and buy her a lot of things."

"What?"

"Oh, ice cream cones, candy, tonic. I bought her some toys. I bought her a doll once. I spent a lot on her."

"What led up to the situation where you killed her?"

After a moment he said, "Well, we got to doing things. Sex, you know? Like the first time, we were in the kitchen. Nobody else was there. My family was over at her family's house. I don't know what came over me, but I just got a feeling. Sex feeling, you know? I got her to put her hand on me. Down here? Well, and then, see, we got to doing that every once in a while when nobody was around."

He stopped but he seemed to have an urge to go on. "Then she told her family about it. She told them what her and James had been doing and they got awful mad about it and her mother talked to my mother. My father came home that night, he'd been drinking, and my mother got mad and she couldn't help it and she let it come out?"

40

He glanced up and I looked at him questioningly.

"Oh," he said, and he laughed nervously. "No, see, my father's name is James, too. And my mother thought it was my father had been fooling around with her. With Kathy? And her parents thought it was him too."

"What did your father say when your mother accused him?"

"First, he got kind of mad. He'd been drinking? I thought he was going to hit her but then he turned, sudden, kind of, and he said, 'Ah, you're all a bunch of damn fools,' and he went into the bedroom and went to sleep."

"What was the situation that caused you to kill the little girl?"

"Well, we were down in the cellar. Of the house where I live? We had been doing it again and when we got finished, she asked me for a nickel so she could get a candy bar. I didn't have a nickel, how could I?"

"I don't know. Why was it that you didn't have one?"

"I was on vacation. From my job. And I spent all the money I had, mostly on her? I told her I'd get one for her—a nickel—but she started to cry and then she started to scream and I tried to shut her up but I couldn't."

"Why was it so important to keep her quiet?"

"Why? Because they were upstairs. The people that had just moved in the downstairs apartment. Below our apartment? They were sitting in their kitchen, just by the door to the cellar, and I knew that. The door was closed but I was afraid they'd hear her and I was afraid she'd go up the stairs, and then when she opened the cellar door they'd see her because I knew the kitchen door was open."

"Why would it have been so bad if they'd seen or heard her?" I asked him.

He glanced up at me, laughed briefly, and then looked away again. "Well, they would of knowed what we'd been doing. She might of told them." He paused. "And, besides, she didn't have any clothes on. I'd gotten her to take them off? So I had to keep her quiet but I didn't know how and I put my hands around her throat—to choke her a little, you know? I didn't want to kill her, just make her quiet, but she wouldn't stop yelling and I grabbed her tighter around the throat and still she wouldn't stop. So I grabbed this cap pistol—she'd brought it down to the cellar with her—and I hit her over the head with it three, four times. Like they do in the movies when they want to knock somebody out for twenty minutes? But it didn't work and I had to do something because she was yelling louder and louder and I knew they'd hear."

His hands were moving faster against each other now and he went on, "I saw the ax, leaning against the wall of the cellar, and I grabbed it because I had to make her be quiet and I took the back—the part that wasn't sharp, you know—and I hit her on the head with that a couple of times. She was quiet and I thought it was all right but then she started yelling again and so I took the blade part and I hit her with that. But I didn't swing it hard. I just dropped it on her, kind of—about so far?" He indicated a distance of about fourteen inches with his hands.

"She was laying on the ground—the dirt floor of the cellar? And, like I said, I dropped it on her, on the back part of her, five times, and then she was still. I looked around, I was expecting them to come down the stairs, and I knew I had to do something so I grabbed this shovel and I started digging. I dug down, a pretty deep hole, and I put her in it. She kind of moaned—crying like. So I took the back of the shovel and hit her over the head with it once hard and then she was quiet for good."

He took a deep breath. "She wouldn't fit—in the hole? So I folded her legs up under her and then she fit good. I began shoveling dirt over her but I wanted to make it nice and solid, so I took this screen—a window screen, it was?—and I put that in the hole and I shoveled more dirt over it. Then I tromped it down good."

He stopped, exhausted.

"What did you do then?"

"I snuck up the stairs," he said. "I got past them, the people who'd just moved into the apartment, and I went in and went in my mother's room. I took off my shoes and got a book and laid down on her bed and tried to read, being natural like? Because I thought my mother would be coming in any minute and I didn't want her to know."

"How did you feel?" I asked him. "Could you read?"

"No, I couldn't. I was afraid I was going to see her, Kathy. Like when you're reborn again—re—re—what? Reincarnation?"

"Do you believe in reincarnation?"

He thought a moment and then said, "I don't know. But I did then. I thought Kathy was going to come into the room, maybe, so I couldn't read. But then after a while I got to feeling awful tired and I went to sleep."

I began asking James La Casse about his childhood.

"What is the earliest thing in your life that you can remember?" I said to him.

"Oh, I don't know," he laughed nervously. "Lots of things. We lived in Renton then."

"What is that, a small town?"

"Yeah, just a little place, you know? They all spoke French there. Well, not everybody, but most. We all did——"

"Your family?"

"Yeah."

"You were born there, in Renton?"

He nodded but was preoccupied with something else. "The earliest thing I can remember?" he said. "It was one day my mother had sent me to the store on the corner for a loaf of bread."

"How old were you?"

"Four? Four and a half, maybe? I was coming back through the alley—the store was on the street behind the house—and two kids that lived in the neighborhood jumped on me and knocked me down and began bashing my head against the ground."

"What did you do?"

"I couldn't do anything. They was a lot bigger than I was, and there was two of them? But then they went away and I got up, all blood, and went into the house."

"Was your mother there?"

He nodded without looking at me.

"What did she do?" I asked him.

"Who? Oh, my mother? Well, she treated me nice. She cleaned me up and she—well, she treated me good. I liked that."

43

"Apart from that incident, how did your mother treat you when you were growing up? Was she usually kind to you, did she sometimes punish you or——"

"Oh no, she never punished me. She was always good to me," James La Casse answered. And then a strange thing happened. He glanced up at me for a second, looked away, and said, "Too good to me. I think she was too good to me. I think that was part of the trouble." Without explaining further, he seemed to indicate that he thought that was one of the factors behind his having killed the little girl.

"I'm not blaming her, I don't mean that," he went on. "It was my own fault. I know that. But anything I did was always all right with her, my mother, you know?"

"Didn't she ever point it out to you when you'd done something wrong?"

"Oh, if I did something real bad she'd cry, she'd cry a little, but she'd always be good to me."

"What was your father like? Did he ever punish you?"

"Oh, no, he never did. He never hit me in his life. He was always awful good to me too."

"And you think that your parents having been so good to you and never having punished you might have had some bearing on your killing the little girl?" I asked.

He nodded vaguely. The flash of possible insight had left him and he did not seem interested in the point any longer.

"How did you get along with other children when you were young, five or six years old?"

This seemed to interest him and he looked up. "Playing with the other kids and such? Well, I don't think they liked me much, you know?"

"Why was that?"

He shrugged, laughing briefly, nervously, and each of his hands rubbed back and forth over the other. "They just didn't like me, I guess. Like when I'd be playing with another kid. If there wasn't nobody else around, he'd play with me, you know? But then if any other kids would come by, he'd go off with them and they wouldn't want me and I'd be alone."

"Were you alone a lot?"

"What?"

"Were you alone a great deal?"

"Well, like I say, if I was playing with a kid and—"

"I know, but did this happen very often?" I asked. "Did you actually end up playing alone a lot of the time?"

"Yeah. Well, not all the time, you know? But most of the time."

"Why do you think it was that the other children didn't like you?"

"I don't know. I was small, smaller than them, maybe that was it. I don't know, they just didn't like me."

"How did you get along in school?"

His eyes lit up. "Oh, good. I got along real good."

"You went to a parochial school, didn't you?"

"No, it was a Catholic school. The sisters. They all liked me. They said I was like a little angel? The way I look, you know?" He touched his cheek uncertainly with his left hand and smiled. He did not look like an angel, but he did not look like a murderer either.

"I did good in school," he said. "I got good grades. Eighties and nineties all the time."

I had checked his prison records. Included were reports from his grammar school teachers. Until the eighth grade, he had always ranked in the upper quarter of his class. One sister had written: "Not only was James a good student in the academic sense, but he was also a model boy, and he never was a disciplinary problem of any kind."

"But then, just after you started school, you moved to the city, didn't you?" I asked him.

He looked surprised that I could know that.

"Yeah, we moved and then I had to learn English. My mother and father, they had to learn too. And I went to a new school? But I did good there too."

"And you had a little brother?"

"Who? Howie? Yeah, he was a couple of years younger than me. Of course, he didn't talk so much then anyway so he didn't have so much trouble learning."

"Did you have many friends after you moved?"

"Some, you know? But like in Renton, the other kids didn't like me much."

"During this period, when you were, say, age six to ten or so, did you ever get mad at any other children? Did you ever lose your temper?"

"No, not very much. Well, yeah, there was one time." He smiled to himself. "I don't know why it was, I don't know what made me do it. It was just after we'd moved, you know? There was this kid lived a couple of doors away from where we moved to? I'd seen him once and the next time I saw him he said 'Hello,' you know? And then he said 'Wait a minute.' He went into a little store, a candy store, and when he came out he had two ice cream cones, a chocolate and a vanilla, and he said, 'Take one, whichever one you want.' He was just trying to make friends, I guess. But I looked at those two ice cream cones and I looked at his face and then—wop! I hit him smack in the nose and he fell down and I ran home."

James La Casse looked up and laughed. "I don't know what made me do it. I saw those ice cream cones and wop! I hit him smack in the nose," he repeated.

After a moment I asked, "Were there any other times when you got mad at other children, hit them?"

"Well, yeah, a few times. You know, when I was younger the other kids were always bigger than me and they'd knock me around. But then when I got to be about ten there were some kids smaller than me. I was still kind of small but there were other kids, younger, still smaller. And I remember a few times, I got hold of one of them and I'd get my hands around his neck and I'd squeeze. Not so's I'd really choke him, you know? But just so he'd turn blue a little."

"Just so he'd turn blue?"

"Yeah. You know. I'd watch his face."

"Did you do this very often?"

"Oh no. Half a dozen times maybe." He was watching his hands moving fast over each other.

"Did you ever get in any trouble with the police during those years?"

"What? Oh. Trouble? No, I was always a good boy. Oh, there was one thing. I was about ten and this kid asked me to go out one night, you know? We went across town to where all these factories were and we were by the side of this one factory, all glass windows? 'Let's throw rocks through the windows,' he says to me. 'No,' I said. 'That's not right. I couldn't do that.' But then he started throwing rocks and I picked up a rock and I started throwing."

James La Casse looked up and said with a slight note of pride in his voice, "I broke eighteen windows."

"You weren't caught?"

He shook his head.

"Did you ever have any relationships with girls during this period?" I asked him.

"You mean in a—in a sex way?"

"Yes."

"No. My mother always told me it wasn't nice, you know?" Then he sat thinking, looking down at the floor to his left. "There was this one time, it wasn't long after I broke those windows. This girl that lived down the street, Elsie. She and me was playing and we went into this old shed. And she started talking about sex things, you know? Then she started to pull up her dress and she said, 'You show me yours and I'll show you mine.' But I wouldn't have anything to do with that and I told her, 'I'm not that kind of boy,' and I ran home."

After a moment I said, "Why was it that you didn't go to high school?"

"Oh, that. I didn't have the money."

"What do you mean?"

"Well, see, I always did good in school. But then in the eighth grade, I got to playing hookey, you know?"

"Why did you do that?"

"Well, there was this other kid. He always wanted to." He shrugged his shoulders. "And I did what he wanted. So, see, my grades were kind of low in the eighth grade because I wasn't there much, you know? And then when the examinations came, in June, I missed some of them so I failed and I couldn't get into high school. They told me to go to this special school for three weeks. During the summer? But it cost ten dollars a week and I couldn't go."

"Why?"

"I didn't have the money. My mother didn't have the money."

"Did you get a job then?"

"Yeah. In this shoe factory? But I didn't like it."

"Why not?"

"Well, this man, this foreman, he kept giving me one job and then another to do and I couldn't finish any one job. And I don't like that. When I start something I like to finish it."

"So you left?"

"After three weeks. But then pretty soon I got another job. In a shoe factory, too. They let me do one thing all the time and that was all right, I liked that job and I had it up until—up until this happened."

It was becoming hot in the room and I went over and opened one barred window.

"They got too much heat in here," he said.

I offered him a cigarette and he took one.

"That's another thing," he said. "I smoke too much. I didn't use to. But I do now?"

"How much do you smoke a day?"

"Oh, a pack, maybe. Well, not quite. But almost. Eighteen maybe. One day I smoked thirty-five. That's the most I ever smoked in one day."

I asked him, "What kind of work does your father do?"

"He's a mechanic, you know? He works on cars. But he can't work too much, only a few days a week, because of the skin trouble he's got."

I had read the reports on James La Casse's father and so I said, "Is the skin trouble due to his drinking?"

"Well, he says it is. But the doctors don't think it is. They don't know why he has it."

"Is it extremely painful to him?"

"Well, yeah. As soon as he takes a drink—of wine or anything?—his skin all breaks out and begins to itch and he has to

48

scratch it. He keeps scratching and then it begins to bleed. But he says he has to have a drink."

"Did your father drink much when you were a little boy?"

"No. No. I don't think he did at all."

"When did he start to drink heavily?"

"I don't know. Well, like about the time I started working, he began drinking wine a lot. He'd drink about a quart a day, maybe two or three of them sometimes. Well, they weren't really quarts, you know. They were—" He indicated with his hands how high the bottles were. "What do you call them?"

He seemed to insist that he get the right name for the bottles. "Fifths?" I said.

"Yeah, that's what they were. Fifths. Not quarts. They were cheap, about fifty cents, maybe fifty-five cents apiece, you know?"

"Did your father drink anything but wine?"

"Oh yeah. Beer and—and whiskey sometimes."

"Did he get drunk often?"

"Well, yeah, kind of. So he couldn't stand up so good, you know?"

"Did your father ever become aggressive, try to hurt anyone, when he'd been drinking?"

"My mother, sometimes. They'd get in fights. Mostly talking fights. But I remember one time, one time he came home, and they got in a fight and he pushed her, against the stove, you know? I ran over and pulled her away—from the stove. And then I stood in front of him and I said, 'Don't you ever do that again.' And he said, 'Who do you think you're talking to?' and he pulled back his arm like to hit me. 'You're not my father!' I said. I don't know what came over me, I never said anything like that before, but he looked at me and then he turned around and went in the other room."

"Did your father ever hit you?"

"No. No, he never did."

"Have you ever had much to drink?" I asked him.

He looked surprised. "No, I couldn't."

"Why couldn't you?"

"Well, the priest."

49

"What do you mean?"

"Before that, when I was nine, we were all at the church, the other kids and me, and the priest asked how many of us would promise before God never to touch a drop of alcohol until we were twenty-one years old. I put up my hand so of course I couldn't drink anything until I was twenty-one."

"As you were growing up, was there any one boy who was a particularly good friend of yours?" I asked him.

"Steve," he answered, as if I should have known.

"You were close friends?"

"Oh, yeah. We did everything together."

"How old were you when you became friends with Steve?"

"Twelve. Yeah, just twelve. We use to do everything together, you know? We even dressed alike. Not all our clothes, I don't mean that. But just some things. Like if he got a pair of white shoes, then I had to have a pair of white shoes. If he got a yellow tie, then I had to have one. Or if he got a western belt—with jewels on it, you know?—then I got one too."

"Did you always get what he had? Or did it sometimes work the other way? Did he sometimes get something to match what you already had?"

"Oh no. It worked both ways. Sometimes I got it first, sometimes he did."

"Did you ever get in a fight with this boy, Steve?" I asked.

"Yeah, once, only once we did."

"How did that happen?"

"We were out hunting. We used to hunt a lot."

"How old were you then?"

"I was fifteen."

"You were working?"

"Yeah, that's how I got the rifle. Steve didn't have a rifle but I had the money because I was working and I bought a rifle. We used to hunt a lot."

"Why did you and he get in a fight?"

"I had this blowgun, a kind of little tube and you could blow BB's through it. No, but that came later. The first thing was we were hunting with my rifle and we saw this squirrel. Steve said for me to shoot it. I didn't want to. But I took aim and shot at it. It was up on the limb of a tree and it just stayed there and I thought I missed it and I was glad. But then it fell down off the branch and it didn't move and it looked dead. I felt awful bad—for having killed it, you know? Then Steve said, 'Cut the tail off it,' but I said I wouldn't. I didn't want to look at it. I walked away and told him to cut the tail off if he wanted to. So he did. But I didn't watch him. Then we started home."

His hands were moving rapidly over each other. He seemed to have finished the story.

"Where did the blowgun come in?" I asked him.

"Oh. Well, we were walking home and I felt kind of funny, kind of all stopped up. Steve was carrying the rifle but I had the blowgun. I took it out and I began blowing BB's through it. And I took aim and I hit Steve in the side of the face with one. He got kind of mad and he threw down the rifle. Then I hit him with one again and he hit me, with his fist. I hit him in the mouth and then I grabbed up the rifle and ran home."

He shook his head. "When I got home I felt real bad, for having hit him like that? So I got out the other blowgun, I had two of them, both the same, and I broke them both in half and threw them away."

"Why did you do that?"

"What?"

"Break them and throw them away."

He looked as if anyone should know the answer to that. "Because it was the blowgun that caused all the trouble," he answered.

"Did you and Steve become friends again?" I said.

"Oh, yes, we never had any more trouble. Except about the shirts, but that wasn't real trouble." I looked at him questioningly and he explained, "After I was about sixteen, I got so I had to wear two shirts, all the time, one over the other? And Steve didn't like it. He kept telling me it was a crazy thing to do and people would think there was something wrong with me if they found out."

"Two white shirts, for example?" I said. "You'd wear one over the other?"

"I had to. I couldn't go out unless I was wearing two. One

buttoned up at the neck and the other over it with a tie. I had to always do that from the time I was sixteen until—until this happened. Summer and winter. And sometimes it got pretty hot in the summer, you know?"

"Why did you have to do it?"

"Well, to make me bigger, to make my chest bigger. I was always kind of small and I wanted to be bigger."

"How would you have felt if you'd been forced to go out with just one shirt?"

"I don't know. I couldn't have. I'd of got so nervous I couldn't have gone out anyway."

I nodded that I understood and then asked, "Around this time, did you go out with girls occasionally?"

"Oh, yeah," he answered. "Go to the show or somewhere, the beach, like that."

"Did you have any one girl friend in particular?"

"Yeah. Monica. She liked me a lot. We used to go out."

"Did you ever have a sexual relationship with her?"

He looked up, not seeming to understand.

"Intercourse," I said.

"No. No. We'd kiss and like that. Neck. But we never went all the way." He laughed briefly. "She kind of tried to once. We were coming home from the show. At night? And we stopped off in this garage. There was nobody there. We began necking and she got kind of hot, you know? And she said, 'Let's go all the way,' but I said, 'No.' I told her I was afraid we'd have a baby and we wouldn't know what to do with it, you know? We wouldn't be able to get married. We wouldn't have any place to live—except with my family and there wouldn't be room with them."

He glanced away, hesitating, and then said, without looking at me, "But that wasn't so much the reason I didn't want to. I didn't want her to have a baby but beside that, the thing was, we hadn't planned it, you know? We'd just come out of the show and been walking home but we hadn't planned it at all. Going all the way, I mean."

"You don't like to do anything unless you've planned it thoroughly?"

"Oh, no," he answered.

"When was the first time," I asked him, "that you ever did anything that you considered to be seriously wrong, against the law?"

"Well, when I robbed the store." His hands began to move fast over each other again. "I needed some money and——" He stopped. "No, that really wasn't the first time. There was something else." Without looking at me, he said, "Once I beat up an old lady, she lived down the block?"

I waited for him to continue and he did. "She was kind of old, fifty or sixty. I heard people talk about her and I knew she had some money. So one night I climbed up the fire escape and went into her apartment. I heard her snoring. It was awful dark but I had a flashlight, you know? I shined it on her face in the bed and she was sleeping. I looked around and I found her bag, her handbag. There was thirty-two dollars in it and I took it and left."

He paused again, then went on. "I got back to my family's apartment and in my room. Then this feeling came over me, a sex feeling? See, I knew a lot of men used to visit her and I got this sex feeling and I had to go back. So I snuck out of the house and went down the block and up the fire escape and into her apartment again. I heard her snoring and she stopped. I went into the bedroom where she was and then she must of seen me because she screamed. I didn't know what to do so I took the flashlight and bashed her on the head with it a few times and she quieted down. I must of knocked her out. I left in a hurry and I went home."

"How did you feel about having done that?"

"Well, I didn't feel anything then except the sex feeling went away, when she screamed? But the next day I felt real bad about it and I wanted to take the money back to her and tell her how sorry I was that I'd hit her over the head. But I didn't dare."

"Why not?"

"Well, my mother. She'd of told my mother and then my mother would of started crying."

"Tell me about this robbery—when you robbed the store," I said.

"It wasn't one. It was two—two stores, the same night."

"Why was it that you decided to rob these stores?"

"Well, it was for the money. I wasn't working for a while and I didn't have any money. And I wanted to take my girl friend—Monica?—and Steve to the show. Not at the same time, you know. But on separate nights. One on Tuesday night and the other on Wednesday. But I didn't have any money. And when I ask somebody to go to the show with me I pay, I don't let them pay, you know?"

"What store did you rob first?"

"This shoe store. A little repair shop like, in the block? In the block where I live? There was a kind of window over the back door, a——"

"Transom?"

"Yeah, I guess. There was an old stepladder in a shed in the alley and I pulled that over and climbed up and let myself in that little window and dropped down. It was awful dark. It was about twelve o'clock at night, you know? I went into the cash register, there was four dollars and twelve cents there, all in quarters and nickels and dimes and pennies, like that. I put it in my pocket and I put a chair on top of a big box and climbed out the way I'd come in, through the little window like, above the door, and I had a pocketful.

"I got out and down the alley and nobody saw me. But that wasn't enough, the four dollars and twelve cents? It wasn't enough because I wanted to buy a shirt too, besides taking Monica and Steve to the show. So I went to this grocery store. Well, it wasn't a grocery exactly, it was a supermarket, a couple of blocks away, where we traded? I got a rock and waited. There was nobody around and I threw it through one of the big glass windows. Then a truck drove around from the back. It must of had the manager in it. I don't know for sure. I was awful scared but I stood right there, I didn't run."

He looked up, momentarily proud for not having run. "Then the truck drove away and I went in through the broken window. It was dark in there and there were a lot of shadows moving around but I didn't know they were shadows. I thought they were people coming at me and I jumped back and waited but there was nobody there. I went into the cash register and there were

54

about thirty-five dollars. I took seven and then I left and went home."

"Why did you take only seven dollars if there were thirty-five there?"

"Well, I knew the manager. We used to trade there? And I didn't want to cause him any more trouble than I had to."

"Just because your family traded there?"

"Well, he was always nice to me."

"Why was it that you took all the money that was in the shoemaker's shop? Why didn't you leave some of his money?"

"He was different. I didn't like him. He did mean things, like once there was a little old dog went into the shop. I saw it. And he kicked him, the dog, he kicked him a lot."

"You had about eleven dollars. What——"

"Eleven dollars and twelve cents."

"What did you do with it?"

"I took Steve to the show one night and Monica the next. And I bought the orange shirt. It was bright orange. Steve had one just like it and that was why I wanted it. It cost five dollars—four dollars and ninety-five cents."

"Were you caught?"

"Yeah, I don't know how. The next week the police came and asked me to come down to the station. They said they knew I did it. Somebody had seen me, they said. So I told them. They took me to the juvenile judge and he put me on probation, for a year?"

"How did your parents act? What did they say?"

"My mother cried a lot."

"Your father?"

"He didn't say anything."

"You didn't get into any other trouble until you killed the little girl?"

"No. No. Well, there was that time when I got caught for kissing the girls. You didn't know about that? It was just before —before the other."

"Just before you killed the little girl?"

He nodded. "See, I was going with Monica, like I said. This one night I was supposed to meet her, in the park? We were going to a show. I was supposed to meet her at seven. I sat down on a bench and waited. But she didn't come. It got to be half past and still she didn't come. Then her sister came and I asked her if she knew where Monica was but she didn't. We got to talking, there was another girl with her, and——"

"How old were these two girls?"

"Monica's sister, she was ten. And the other one, she lived in the neighborhood, she was eleven, I think."

"And you were about eighteen then?"

"Yeah."

"What did you and the two girls do?"

"Well, we got to talking and fooling around. It didn't look like Monica was going to come. It was about eight o'clock, you know? So I asked them if they'd like to have a coke. We went into this drugstore and I ordered three cokes. Of course, I didn't drink mine but——"

"Why didn't you?"

"What?"

"Drink your coke?"

"Oh, I never drink coke. I just order it so as—well, you know—you got to order something."

"But why didn't you drink it?"

"Oh, I never drink coke. Too much acid. I don't like anything with acid."

"Then what happened with the two girls?"

"Well, they drank the cokes and we were talking and then we went out and down the street. It was getting dark, see, and we were fooling around and we went into this shed. I don't know, we were just kidding around, and Sylvia, that's Monica's sister, she asked me if I ever kissed Monica. I told her sure, lots of times, and then, I don't know, I was just fooling, you know? I asked them if they'd like me to kiss them. I kissed Sylvia and then I kissed the other one. They wanted me to keep on and they asked me to kiss them again but then their mother—Sylvia's mother—called for her from across the street. I told them they'd better go home and I'd wait in the shed till later and then I'd leave. I told them not to say anything to their mothers about what we'd been doing because they wouldn't like it."

"But the police did find out, didn't they?"

"Well, yeah, but first her brother, Sylvia's brother, found out. She must of told him. Because the next day he came up to me and grabbed me and said, 'I hear you been fooling around with my sister.'

" 'Which one?' I said, because, see, I was going with Monica but it was Sylvia I'd been fooling around with the night before. 'Don't give me that,' he said. 'I hear you been fooling around with Sylvia.'

" 'Me?' I said. 'Not me.' He was a great big guy. He was in the marines and he was home on furlough? But I didn't know that. I didn't know it the night before or I wouldn't of kissed Sylvia.

" 'I ought to clean up the street with you,' he said. 'If you were a little bigger I would.'

" 'I'm only fifteen,' I said. Of course I was eighteen, but I'm kind of small and I thought maybe he'd believe me. He let go of me and he said, 'Well, don't ever let me catch you playing around with her again and stay away from the house.'

"I asked him if I couldn't come to see Monica because I was going with her and he said not for a while, anyway. But then the next day the police came and got me again and took me to the judge. The other girl must of told her parents too and I admitted it but all I'd been doing was kissing them. So the judge told me not to do it again and let me go."

"And this was just before you killed the little girl?" I asked him.

"Yeah."

After James La Casse had told me of his relationship with the four-year-old Kathy and of how he had killed her, he had gone on to explain that in order to throw suspicion away from himself, he helped the police search for the body. I checked what he told me with the police and found his story to be substantially correct.

He said, "The morning after I—after I hit her with the ax, I was in the apartment alone. There was this knocking at the door. It was the police. I thought they came to get me but they just wanted to see the cellar of the house. They asked me if I had a key and I said yes and I took them down the stairs.

"I took them into the cellar and showed them around. Then this lieutenant—of the police?—he asked me, 'How come it's so clean down here?'

"'I just cleaned it all up a couple of weeks ago,' I said and that was right. I had cleaned it up all nice the first day my vacation started. Well, he—the lieutenant?—he began looking around, stomping on the ground. 'There any soft spots?' he asked me. 'No, I don't think so,' I answered him.

"Then he went over to the spot where I'd—where I'd buried her and he looked down and stepped on it and then he said to the other police, 'Let me have that shovel'—the same one I'd used before, you know?—and he began digging. I stood there watching him. Then he came to that screen I'd put in. 'What's this?' he said and he pulled it up. 'You know why this is here?' he asked me.

"'Yeah,' I said. 'I put it there. See, when I cleaned up the cellar, I wanted to get it out of the way. So I buried it there. I figured that would be a good place to keep it and then if we ever needed it we could just dig it up.'

"'Oh,' this lieutenant said, and then he began putting the dirt back over the screen, filling up the hole."

James La Casse grinned and shook his head. He went on. "Then he started looking again. 'There any more soft spots around here?' he asked me.

"'Yeah, over there in the corner, I think there's one,' I said. You know, kind of playing along with him? He began digging over there in the corner but of course he didn't find anything. And then they left."

"What happened after that?" I asked him.

"Well, that day I could see them from the house—the police cars—driving around the neighborhood, looking for her. After supper they began getting up a searching party and my father and me, we helped search. There was about a dozen of us, police and fellows from the neighborhood. We were looking through the brush out on the edge of town."

"And you were acting as if you were helping them?"

He looked up. "Oh, yeah. I was tearing through the bushes, looking everywhere. 'I think there's something over here,' I called to them one time. But it really wasn't anything. Throw suspicion away from myself, you know? We didn't find her, of course.

"Then the next day, the police came to the house again and they said they wanted me to come down to the station. They said it wasn't much important, they just wanted to ask me a few questions. But I knew something was up. Then when they got me down there they put me in this little room. 'Now, we know you did it,' one of them, a detective, I guess, said to me. 'You might as well tell us.'

"'Did what?' I answered him. Well, they kept at me, but I wouldn't admit to anything. 'I don't know nothing about it,' I told them. Then this one detective, he took me in another room and he said, 'Now, you're a Catholic and I'm a Catholic and us Catholics have got to confess things like this. It's the only way we feel better. Now, you can tell me, what did you do with her? Are you holding her somewhere? Is she still alive? Or is she dead——'

"When he said 'dead,' I don't know, something came over me and I told him, 'I'm the one. I did it.'"

I talked to the police who had worked on the case. Photographs of the murdered girl used at the trial showed eighteen ax cuts on her body as against the five James La Casse said he had inflicted. The photographs indicated that La Casse had lost control of himself completely and had had a tremendous outburst of aggression against the girl.

Psychiatrists examined La Casse and found that although he was maladjusted in many respects, he was not psychotic. He waived trial by jury and was sentenced to life imprisonment in the state penitentiary without possibility of parole.

Of interest is the fact that just before James La Casse committed the murder, at the time he had kissed the two girls

aged ten and eleven, the juvenile court judge had decided that
La Casse should be examined by a state psychiatric board in
order to determine whether he was a sexual psychopath. But the
board's schedule was so heavy that his case could not be
considered until the following month. The judge continued him
on probation. And, meanwhile, La Casse murdered the four-year-
old girl.

After having interviewed La Casse, I went to the home of
his parents. They lived in a small clean tenement. I rang one of
the rusted, outside bells several times and there was no answer.
I went into a barren hall. A small girl peered out of a door and
I asked her where the La Casses lived. She pointed to the
apartment above the one she was in and stood watching me.
I went up the stairs and knocked on the door. No answer. I
knocked several times but still there was no answer. As I started
down the stairs, I heard a door open.

"Yes? What is it?" a man called in a French accent.

"Are you Mr. La Casse?"

"Yes."

"I've been talking to your son at the state prison. I'd like
to talk to you if it's convenient."

"Sure. Come up."

I went back up the stairs and La Casse held the door for
me. He was a small man, about fifty years old, and although
it was early afternoon he looked as if he had just gotten up.

The door led into the kitchen. "Sit down," he said, indicating
a chair by the white enamel kitchen table. On the table was a
cup of cocoa and two bologna sandwiches.

"I was just going to have a little food," La Casse said,
sitting down.

"I thought probably no one was home."

"I was sleeping and I just got up and I wasn't dressed right,"
he said apologetically.

La Casse was dressed in a rumpled, dirty shirt and trousers,
his face was broken out in red splotches, and he needed a shave
badly. He seemed to be a mild-mannered man, eager to please.

"See, I have to sleep during the day," he said. He put

his fingers to one cheek. "This skin trouble I got, it keeps me from sleeping all night. I don't sleep a wink all night and then during the day I get so tired I got to sleep." He waved his hands to indicate helplessness.

"Yes, your son told me you had skin trouble." I went on to explain who I was and the purpose of my visit. I asked him if Mrs. La Casse were home.

"No. She works, at the mill. See, I can't work with this skin. I haven't worked in over a year, since—since the boy got in trouble."

"I had hoped I could talk to Mrs. La Casse, too. About your son."

He shook his head. "She won't talk to anybody about that. I don't mind, it's all right with me, but she wouldn't talk to you."

I asked him what kind of a boy his son James had been.

"Quiet, awful quiet," he said. "Too quiet. Anything bothered him, he never said a word. Just go into his room."

"Were you and Mrs. La Casse pretty strict with him?"

La Casse gave a laugh. "Strict? No, too much the other way. Anything he wanted, we let him have. Anything he did, we never said anything to him. I mean, he never tried to do anything really bad. But still——" He sat back and looked up at the ceiling. "We talked about it a lot, the wife and me, since he got in that trouble. We were too easy with him. We think that was part of it. But what could we do? We thought we were doing the best thing, at the time. I could never hit him." He shook his head. "I just couldn't."

"Did he ever get mad, as a boy, lose his temper?"

"No. He was always quiet. Sometimes he'd cry. I remember many a time he'd sit at this table and try to do his lessons and cry."

"Why was that?"

"Well, he was a smart boy, he did good in school. But he always wanted to be the best, the top of the class. It was reading he had some trouble with. He couldn't get some of the words. We spoke French until we moved here and we didn't know a lot of those words. He'd sit at this table and he'd ask us what some of them were and we didn't know and there was nobody around here we could ask. And if he couldn't get them all, he'd put his head down on his arms and cry. He did pretty good in school but he always wanted to do better."

"Was your son an exceptionally clean child?" I asked.

"Clean? He thought of nothing else. Always when he was a kid, but it got worse and worse. The last couple of years before he got in trouble, it was something. He'd shave four, five times a day. He'd wash his hands every ten minutes he was in the house. And he'd stand in front of that mirror and take a half-hour combing his hair."

"He was very particular about his clothes, wasn't he?"

"Was he? That last couple of years he had to have four clean shirts a day. Four. He always wore two, one under the other. He had to have one clean one for underneath and he'd change the outside one three times every day—morning, noon, and night. My wife was working and I did the washing and she did the ironing. I tell you that was a lot of work doing those four shirts for him every day."

"But you never said anything to him?"

La Casse waved his hands. "No. We should of, I guess. But we just did them for him."

"About your skin trouble," I said. "Has it been getting worse?"

"Well, it's about the same. I had it before, before the boy got in trouble but not so bad. But after that, it got real bad and it stays that way. A little wine makes it worse. But my nerves, you know, I get so jumpy and I have to take a little wine and then it gets worse."

"Have you been to a doctor?"

"Doctor? I go to the hospital. Three days a month. When I'm there it gets better. They don't know what it is. They don't know what to do for it but it gets better. One doctor there, he says it's because I get away from here. He says I see those people across the street every day—the mother and father of the little girl, the one he killed—and that makes it worse."

"Do they speak to you?"

He shook his head. "They think we're some kind of—of

animals. I don't know, maybe they're right. But the doctor says to move away where we won't—you know, be reminded of it. But I tell him, how can I? We haven't got any money to move."

He touched his face gingerly. "I'm going to the hospital again day after tomorrow. I've got to shave. See, the reason I don't shave, it makes it worse, makes the skin worse. But I got to shave to go to the hospital."

"Well, you could go without shaving."

He shook his head. "I got some pride left. I may be poor and have a boy——" He stopped. "But I want to look decent when I go out. That's why I never go out except to the hospital. Shaving."

"Besides the little girl's parents, how do the other people in the neighborhood act toward you?"

"You mean since the boy got in that trouble? Some speak to us, some don't. About half and half. Of course, those that do speak to you, you don't know what they're really thinking. It bothers my wife more than it does me. I tell her it doesn't make any difference. But she gets to feeling bad about it."

After we had been talking for an hour, I thanked him and got up to leave. He didn't seem to want to be alone.

"Look," he said. "Look in here." He took me into the living room, which also served as his wife's and his bedroom. "These things. All presents he gave us."

He showed me a large jewel box made of matchsticks glued together. "He paid ten dollars for that. And look at this." He pointed to a ceramic bust of Christ. "He was always giving us things like that. We told him to save his money but——" He waved his hands.

Then he said, "You want to see his room?"

"Yes."

He led me back through the kitchen and into the third room of the apartment. It was a small bedroom almost fully taken up by a double bed. On the wall was a Harvard pennant.

He pointed to another ceramic figure of Christ. There were holes where the eyes should have been. "Look," he said, "it lights up." He pushed the switch and the eyes lit up electrically. They gave the impression that they were watching you no matter where you were in the room.

"He had to have that," La Casse said. "It cost twenty-seven dollars and ninety-five cents, I think it was. A lot of money. But he had to have it."

We went back into the kitchen.

"Where is the bathroom?" I asked. "In the hall?"

La Casse nodded and then turned and looked in the bedroom. On the far side of the bedroom was a sealed door with a transom above it.

"The bathroom's out there," he said. "The other side of that door. You get on a chair in the bathroom and you can look through there and into the bedroom. When he was a kid, him and his brother, I used to some nights get up on a chair and look in, to see if they were doing anything funny. Sex, you know. But they never were."

"Did you or your wife ever talk to them about sex when they were growing up?"

La Casse shook his head. "No, we should of, I guess. But we didn't. We couldn't talk about things like that. We just couldn't."

I went out in the hall, thanked him, and began to say goodby.

"You know, it's funny," he said. "It's hard to understand things. Like when he was a kid. We had two little turtles. In a jar. In the kitchen there. We had to feed them something and I used to catch flies and give them to them. This one day he comes in, from the school I guess it was, and he saw me giving the flies to those turtles and he got awful upset. He cried and cried and we couldn't stop him. He kept saying over and over, 'Little flies have got as much right to live as anything.'"

La Casse shook his head. "I don't get it. He got so upset over a few flies being killed but then he didn't think anything of killing a little girl. The same night after he killed her—we didn't know it of course—but I remember, he sat in there and ate his supper just as calm as could be. I don't get it."

64

Some months later I returned to the home of James La Casse's parents. My aim was to interview his mother although Mr. La Casse and the prison administrators had said they did not think she would talk to me. On the way, I checked through the schedule which had been filled out from information in the prison files. The latest reports of the prison psychologists indicated that La Casse was not considered psychotic. However, they did indicate an extreme compulsive tendency, as is obvious from what has already been said about him. His over-all I.Q. was 82, usually classified as dull normal.

Mr. and Mrs. La Casse were both at home. Mr. La Casse remembered me and introduced me to his wife. She was a short, stocky woman who smiled considerably. She did not seem aggressive or resentful because I had come. I explained briefly the nature of the study and asked her if she would be willing to answer some questions about both her sons. She agreed, and for the next two hours I asked her the questions on the interview schedules. She was certainly quite co-operative, and naturally it crossed my mind that her husband and the prison administrators had been positive she would not be. People are often in error about such matters as these.

Mrs. La Casse felt that James' birth was much more difficult for her than that of his control brother. Forceps were used in the case of James, not in the case of his brother. The forceps left indentations on the back of his head which are discernible today. James was born with a defective genital organ; he could not urinate. An operation to make urination possible was performed the day after he was born. (The above has been verified by checking other sources.)

When he was one year old, James had a series of convulsions, Mrs. La Casse said. They lasted about a week. Mrs. La Casse was extremely worried, a doctor was consulted, and then the matter was dropped. As previously noted, at age four James was severely beaten by two older boys. Two years later, James was hit squarely on the back of the head by a rock thrown by another boy and knocked unconscious.

James' brother, according to Mrs. La Casse, did not have

any serious illnesses, operations, or accidents during his early years of life.

James seemed to her always to have been more sensitive to criticism or the threat of it than his brother. She remembered that James had been concerned about his small size while his brother had not had that problem.

It would be premature to present any detailed analysis of this case. That will be done with cases considered later, after more of the findings of the study have been explicated. However, there are certain aspects of James La Casse's environment and personality which can be pointed to as being of possible importance and significance: La Casse was subjected to an array of physical and psychological frustrations in early life. Also, his parents did little to train him effectively to follow the approved behavioral patterns of the society. Yet, his mother was in a sense an overly moral woman. And she tended to cry when he did something of which she disapproved. Both parents were abnormally repressed about sexual matters.

James La Casse generally held his aggression within to an abnormal degree. Yet on infrequent occasions, prior to the murder, he would become violently aggressive when frustrated. Further, and as his compulsive behavior indicates, he had extreme guilt feelings, especially with respect to his sexual behavior.

These factors, then, may be some of the keys to the problem of why individuals commit murder. In further chapters and case studies, we shall consider the significance of them and of still other factors.

3. Physical Frustration

MURDERERS seem to be people who have experienced a great deal of physical pain in early life due to serious illnesses, operations, accidents, and beatings. The fifty-one murderers in the group studied here were, according to the mothers, subjected to physical frustrations to a much greater extent than were their control brothers.

It is obvious that physical frustrations frequently lead to, and have bound up with them, a strong component of psychological frustration. In a given individual's total being, the two are inseparable. However, for purposes of analysis, they must be treated separately. In this chapter, physical frustration will be considered. Psychological frustration will be analyzed in the next chapter.

Following the previously mentioned frustration-aggression hypothesis of Dollard and his colleagues, the tentative assumption is made here that physical frustration leads to a build-up of aggressive feelings within the individual. And it is logical to assume further that the earlier in the life development of the individual this frustration occurs, the more likely it is to lead to repressed aggression which may later explode outwardly. The earlier the frustration occurs, the less is the individual equipped with the language tools which will enable him to deal with the aggression at a conscious level.

First, the matter of whether the mothers considered the births of their sons to have been physically difficult for them, the mothers, was investigated. This was based on the belief that if the births were especially difficult for the mothers, they were also frustrating to the infants.

Twenty-eight of the fifty-one mothers reported that the births of their murderer sons were especially difficult while only nine of the mothers reported that the births of the control brothers were difficult. This leads to a statistical relationship which is highly significant. (Using a two-by-two table, $X^2 = 15.310$, $P < 0.01$.)

Some scoff at the idea that what happens at the birth of a child can influence his later personality. I do not. This is not to say that these factors inevitably lead to particular personality characteristics but rather that they are frequently contributing influences.

Many of the mothers said that the weeks just before the birth of the murderers, the periods of the births themselves, and the weeks following the births were exceedingly trying for them. They stressed the extreme labor pains they had experienced, as compared with the births of their other sons. (Incidentally, none of the 102 births was by Caesarean operation.) They implied, in some cases, that the difficult births had set up a chain of negative circumstances in their relationships with their murderers-to-be sons:

"Everything went wrong with that child from the first, I tell you. When I had him I was in awful pain. We had to call the doctor and he couldn't—you know, get him out. There was something went wrong, I guess, I don't know what. He cried all the time, he couldn't eat good, and he was forever getting into trouble, falling off something, disappearing under my very eyes. I don't know what was the matter with him. He was a good child in some ways, he was nice to you but then something would always be coming up. I had more trouble with him than all the others put together."

"I don't know why it was but that was the only one where the birth was hard on me. He came out backwards for one thing, the woman we had said. We had a—what do you call it? —a midwife woman to help out. . . . No, his legs was all right but he was the fussiest of the three. I'll say he was fussy. Always sick with something and no money for doctors. I was so weak with him I got the pneumonia. . . . Oh, he was about four months and he got it too. Me and him laid up and the other one just starting to run around. I wouldn't want to go through it again, I tell you. And then when he was four he got the rheumatic fever and he never got over it if you ask me. But would he do what I tell him? It was the blood as near as I can figure it out."

It seemed quite apparent that some of the mothers had developed unconscious aggressive feelings toward those sons with whom they had experienced extreme difficulty in giving birth. Then, as the sons passed through infancy and childhood, the mothers, without realizing it, unduly frustrated them. The children in turn became difficult, aggressive. The mothers frustrated the children further. And the snowball of frustration-aggression interaction grew larger and larger.

A majority of the births of the murderers and their brothers occurred in the late 1920's or early 1930's. Some of their families were without the advantage of hospital facilities. Because of lack of funds or in the belief that a doctor was unnecessary, physicians were frequently not called to the home unless complications arose. Often the mothers relied on midwives.

Nevertheless, the mothers reported that in the births of nine murderers and no brothers forceps were used by physicians with severe external effects, ranging from a torn mouth to a lacerated ear to marked head indentations. Four of the nine defects were permanent in the sense that they could readily be seen when the individual entered adulthood.

A primary example of a murderer with a marked effect of forceps is the previously mentioned James La Casse. He has a definite indentation in the back of his head which several sources have specified as being due to the use of forceps at delivery. Again, no one can sensibly claim that one experience, such as the misuse of forceps, will lead inevitably to murder. However, one such experience may be a small but definite contributing factor which when added to many other frustration-causing factors may exert strong influence toward murder.

Some of the murderers and their brothers were born with severe physical defects which were not due to the birth process itself or to forceps. An example here is an abnormally large head. These defects did not appear to cause the individuals physical pain. However, they frequently caused them embarrassment. Therefore, such defects will be considered in the chapter which deals with psychological frustration.

A serious operation is defined here as one where major surgery is involved. Such operations performed prior to the age of twelve years were definitely more prevalent in the cases of the murderers than their brothers. There was a total of twenty-three operations carried out on the 102 individuals. Nineteen of these operations, or about 83 per cent, were performed on the murderers, while four, or about 17 per cent, were performed on the control brothers. As Table 5 in Appendix A indicates, the relationship is statistically significant.

The types of operations included serious appendectomies, operations on the genital organs, and heart surgery. It is of some importance to note that, in the cases of the murderers, the largest single category of operations was composed of surgery on the genital organs. (This does not include normal circumcision.) There were five murderers so operated upon. None of the brothers experienced an operation of this type.

Circumcision operations were investigated separately from these major operations. Here, there were no significant differences between the murderers and their brothers. A few more of the murderers than of the brothers were circumcised, according to the mothers' reports: twenty-eight murderers as compared to twenty-four brothers. And there was a slight tendency for the murderers to have been circumcised earlier in life than the brothers. But these differences are not statistically significant.

According to the mothers, the murderers experienced a considerably greater number of serious illnesses prior to the age of twelve than did their brothers. By serious illnesses are meant those more severe than the usual, "normal" childhood diseases and illnesses. Illnesses directly due to accidents are not included; they will be considered later.

Thirty-seven of the murderers experienced one or more serious illnesses before twelve years of age; fifteen of the control brothers fell into this category. Among the thirty-seven murderers there were sixty-six illnesses while among the fifteen brothers there were seventeen illnesses. Thus the murderer group experienced serious illnesses about four times as frequently as did the control group. Table 6, Appendix A, shows these results.

A truly startling point is that in the cases of fourteen murderers there was evidence of epilepsy of some degree as against only one case among the brothers. (See Table 1 for a complete classification of the illnesses.)

Table 1

Types of Serious Illnesses Experienced by Murderers and Control Brothers before Age 12

	Number of Cases among Murderers	Number of Cases among Brothers
Epilepsy	14	1
Severe Measles	11	5
Severe Pneumonia	9	4
Whooping Cough	7	2
Scarlet Fever	4	2
Severe Intestinal Difficulty	3	0
Other *	18	3
Total	66	17

---

* No specific illness included here occurred more than twice in either group.

As Table 1 shows, over twice as many murderers as control brothers had severe cases of measles during their early lives.

Similarly, the murderers outnumbered their brothers by over two to one with respect to severe cases of pneumonia and whooping cough.

Why this great preponderance of illness in the cases of the murderers? Perhaps they were constitutionally inferior to their brothers and therefore more prone to contract diseases. More likely, the explanation may lie in the fact that the murderers had at birth and in the years immediately following been subjected to anxiety-inducing experiences to a greater degree than the brothers. And the necessity to cope with the anxiety may have lowered the murderers' resistances to germs and also made them more prone to organic disorders. In addition, I believe that illnesses in themselves cause frustration and anxiety which in turn lead to a build-up of aggression in the individuals concerned.

The case of a boy named Anthony Bianco comes to my mind as an apt example of a murderer who has a history of a number of serious illnesses. His parents were poor, had little money for medical attention. At the age of eight months, Anthony had whooping cough. At fourteen months, he had measles but it was not an unduly severe case. When two years old, he contracted chicken pox; he had at this time an extremely high fever for one week. (Prolonged high fevers in early life seem to be common among murderers, incidentally.)

Anthony's mother said that she thought him to be a very nervous boy. Beginning at age three he had continual digestive difficulties and ate little. When he was six years old, Anthony's liver became seriously enlarged, and he was confined to bed for five months.

The boy developed a peptic ulcer at age twelve. The ulcer caused him considerable pain for at least the next three years. Also, when he was twelve, Anthony was hit by an automobile. No bones were broken and it was believed that he had not suffered a severe concussion. However, he was badly shaken up, to say the least.

When Anthony was fifteen, he made a sexual attack on a little girl. She screamed and he beat her to death. He was sentenced to life imprisonment.

The illnesses which befell the thirty-seven murderers tended to occur earlier in life than did those which befell the fifteen control brothers. Eleven of the murderers contracted a serious illness during the first year of life while none of the brothers did so. Even at ages over one year the brothers tended to contract illnesses later in life than did the murderers. This provides some support for my contention that the earlier in life does a frustrating experience occur, the more weight does it have and the more likely is it to lead to violent aggressive action at a later time.

I thought originally that starvation and near suffocation might be frustrating situations of significance in the early lives of the murderers. But this turned out not to be the case. The mothers reported that only three of the murderers and one of the control brothers had gone without food for one or more periods of over twenty-four hours during infancy and early childhood. With respect to suffocation, only two of the murderers and one of the brothers were said by the mothers to have almost died due to lack of air.

The number and kinds of serious accidents which befell the murderers and their brothers during the first twelve years of their lives were investigated. Serious accidents were defined, with one exception, as those which required professional medical attention. The exception was falling on the head. Any fall from a place about six feet or more high was considered serious if the child landed on his head. The reason for this was that such falls frequently cause no external effects and so no medical attention is sought by the parents.

A significantly greater number of murderers than of their brothers presumably experienced frustration due to the physical (and psychological) pain which resulted from accidents. Of the twenty-nine accidents reported, twenty-three, or 79 per cent, happened to twenty of the murderers; the remaining six accidents befell six of the control brothers. (See Table 7 in Appendix A for the chi-square figure.)

A rather amazing point is that eleven of the murderers

fell down flights of stairs or fell from trees or other relatively high places once or more and landed on their heads. (See Table 2 for a full classification of the accidents.) According to the mothers, none of the control brothers had such falls. I think this may be of first-rank importance. The impact of the fall may cause some disarrangement of the nervous system which in turn may bring about a lessening of aggression control by the individual. At the same time, the frustration which results from the fall and its effects may contribute to a build-up of aggression within the child.

Table 2

Types of Serious Accidents Occurring to Murderers and Control Brothers before Age 12

	Number of Cases among Murderers	Number of Cases among Brothers
Fell on Head	13	0
Broke Arm or Leg	2	3
Wounded by Instrument *	3	1
Hit by Car **	3	0
Bitten by Animal	2	0
Other	0	2
Total	23	6

---

* By scissors, knife, etc.
** Severe lacerations but head was not hit and no limbs were broken.

A majority of the thirteen falls occurred during the first two years of life of the murderers. The infant was on the floor or in a carriage near the top of a flight of stairs. He crawled to the top stair, or the carriage tipped, and he fell to the bottom, striking his head severely. The factor that struck me about these incidents is that the mothers were usually near by but seemed *to allow* the accidents to happen, as is implied in their comments:

74

"I put the carriage by the head of the stairs because it was hot and there was a nice cool breeze there and I didn't think it would tip over."

"He was by the head of the stairs but—well, he could crawl a little but I didn't think he'd ever get over to them and tumble down like he did."

"He was always getting into trouble, falling like that. He should of knowed better. I had the other kid to take care of and I couldn't be watching him all the time. How could I put one of them little fences up? We didn't have nothing like that."

One of the murderers fell down a flight of eighteen stairs three times before the age of one and a half. I talked to this man's mother at length. She was a woman of about sixty, pleasant, and, I would judge, above average in intelligence.

"Did your son ever have any accidents as a child?" I asked her.

"No, I don't believe so," she answered.

"Did he ever cut himself badly, ever get hit by a car, fall from a tree, fall downstairs, anything like that?"

"Well, yes, as a matter of fact, he did. He fell down them stairs out there. It hasn't crossed my mind for years."

"How old was he when he fell down the stairs?"

"Oh, about a year. But, you see, he fell down them—well, it was three times, it was."

"How old was he the first time?"

"Just less than a year, I'd of said. Yes, about ten months."

"How did it happen that he fell?"

"Well, he was crawling around a little, then. He was away from the stairs and I didn't think he could crawl so far. But the next thing I knew he was yelling something fierce and I found him there at the bottom. I'll show you. It's the same stairs."

She went out of her apartment and into the middle of the

second floor of the small tenement. I followed her. There were eighteen stairs and they were steep.

"Could you tell at the time how badly he hurt himself?"

"Not much, I guess."

"How did he act?"

"Well, after he stopped crying he was quiet for a while."

"How long was he quiet?"

"Oh, for a couple of days, he was kind of peculiar quiet."

She told me about the other two times when her son fell down the stairs. They happened in the few months following the first occurrence. But she seemed to have no conscious understanding of the fact that the falls could have any significance.

The mothers were asked questions concerning whether they or their husbands struck hard or beat severely the murderers and control brothers. (Spanking is not included here.) They were also asked how old the children were when first beaten and how frequently the beatings occurred. It is of course possible that the mothers de-emphasized instances where they themselves beat their children. However, a number of the mothers were quick to admit that they had beaten their sons severely.

As one mother said, "He was always getting into trouble. I shouldn't have done it, I suppose, but I'd get so mad at him I'd pick up a stick or anything I could get my hands on and lay into him. Once I beat him real bad."

Another mother said, "I remember one time I got so upset with him I took this poker we had for the stove and I hit him with that. I kind of lost control of myself and I couldn't stop."

A slightly greater number of murderers than control brothers were beaten by the mothers: twenty-two murderers as compared to sixteen brothers. But the beatings began at approximately the same ages in the cases of both murderers and brothers: usually between the ages three and six. There were no important differences in the frequency with which mothers beat the murderers and the brothers. On the average, they beat the twenty-two murderers, and the sixteen brothers as well, about once every six months. However, four of the murderers and two of the brothers were beaten once a week or more often.

The fathers (and stepfathers) struck hard or beat severely twenty-three of the murderers and fourteen of the brothers. The murderers were slightly younger than the brothers when the fathers first beat them. The fathers beat the murderers and the brothers about once every three months, somewhat more frequently than did the mothers. According to the mothers, therefore, neither they nor the fathers generally beat the sons to what could be termed a tremendous extent. However, when they did beat them, the beatings were often extremely severe. This was especially true with respect to the fathers.

A spry little old woman said in talking about her husband and her murderer son, "He beat him once, I thought the boy was done for. Oh, I'd hit them pretty hard on occasion but nothing like that. This time his father just lost his head. He knocked that boy from one end of the house to the other. Beating him. Beating him. He was like a man gone insane, my husband."

"Before that," I asked, "had your husband seemed to like the other children better than John?" John was the murderer.

"Liked? Well, I don't know how he liked them. But John was the one he got mad at the most. Of course, John was always—well, he was a peculiar child. Always getting into trouble and yet you'd never know it until he'd done it. But that was no excuse for the way his father beat him that time.

"I can still remember it to this day, the way he beat him. There was blood on the wall, I can see it now."

"How did John act toward his father after that?"

The mother drew herself up, in a sense proudly. "Never spoke to him again. Never. Except as he had to. If his father asked him something, he'd answer. But that was all."

"How old was John when this happened?"

"He was—he was six. He'd just started school."

Perhaps it was coincidence, perhaps it was not. But when he was twenty-four years old, John beat to death a man thirty years older than himself.

About three times as many murderers as control brothers were beaten severely once or more by people other than their parents: nineteen murderers and six brothers. These other people included uncles, older brothers, unrelated men, or adolescent boys in the neighborhood. The remaining thirty-two murderers and forty-five brothers were not beaten in this way, to the best of the mothers' knowledge. These differences are statistically significant at the one per cent level. ($X^2 = 8.954$; two-by-two table used.)

During the course of the research, an Index of Physical Frustration was developed. This index utilizes most of the more or less specific types of presumed physical frustration which have previously been enumerated in this chapter. The index pertains only to physical frustrations which the individual has experienced during the first twelve years of life.

One point is allotted for:

1. A difficult birth.
2. Serious effects of forceps at birth.
3. Each serious operation.
4. Each serious illness.
5. Each serious accident.
6. Each serious beating by someone other than a parent or stepparent.
7. One or more serious beatings by the mother.
8. One or more serious beatings by the father or stepfather.

The higher the index score, the greater the physical frustration in early life is taken to be. The minimum score is zero but there is no maximum limit. The reader may ask, why assign the equal weight of one point to each serious operation, illness, accident, beating, and the like when it is obvious that differing degrees of frustration were involved? The reason for assigning one point to each is that there is no especially reliable way to distinguish systematically among the amounts of resultant frustration. In the behavioral sciences at present, we usually have to employ broad-gauge, rough-and-ready measures. But those measures are far better than none at all.

The Index of Physical Frustration scores are significantly higher for the fifty-one murderers than for the fifty-one control brothers. (See Table 3.) In fact, the differences are strikingly great: twenty-five of the murderers have scores of four or less, while fifty of the brothers have scores of four or less. Conversely, twenty-six of the murderers have scores of five or more, while only one brother has a score that high. The mean score for the fifty-one murderers is 4.53; for the fifty-one brothers the mean score is 1.65, indicating a tremendous difference.

Table 3
*Scores of Murderers and Control Brothers on Index of Physical Frustration **

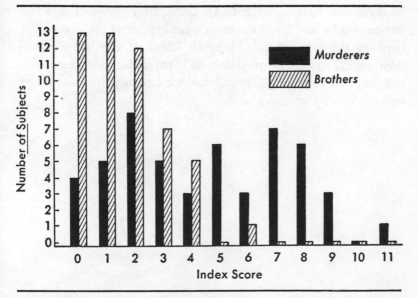

* Total number of murderers = 51. Total number of brothers = 51. Using a two-by-six table (scores 5 through 11 combined for the calculation), $X^2 = 33.102$; $P < 0.01$.

The index scores of the pairs of murderers and their brothers were analyzed. Forty of the murderers had scores higher than their brothers. In the cases of seven pairs, the scores of the murderers and their brothers were equal. And in the remaining four pairs the scores of the murderers were lower than those of their brothers. There were, then, eleven murderers who did not have index scores higher than those of their respective control brothers. In some of these cases, the murderer had experienced much greater *psychological* frustrations than his brother, thus causing the over-all amount of his frustration to outweigh that of the brother.

However, if the mothers were reporting accurately, there can be little doubt that, in the cases of the fifty-one murderers and fifty-one control brothers studied here, the murderers were *as a group* subjected in childhood and adolescence to an overwhelmingly greater amount of physical frustration than were the brothers. In the next chapter, the psychological frustrations experienced by the murderers and their brothers will be enumerated. An Index of Psychological Frustration will be employed to provide a measure of the differences between the two groups. Then, an Index of General Frustration, which combines physical and psychological frustration, will be used to distinguish still further between the murderers and the control brothers.

The Case of Arlin Redfern

ARLIN REDFERN was eighteen years old, worked intermittently on a road-repair crew. He drank heavily at times and
had a police record of some length. He had spent a year in a
reformatory for stealing from a department store. He had been
on probation because of another instance of theft.

On a night in midwinter, Redfern visited a middle-aged
prostitute, Lizzie Howard, whom he had visited several times
before. This time, after having had a sexual relationship with
her, he attempted to steal money from her. Lizzie Howard
resisted and he stabbed her at least a dozen times with a kitchen
knife, hit her twice with a flatiron.

Redfern then fled through the snow. The next morning,
Lizzie Howard was found by a neighbor, still alive. She was
standing in the doorway of her apartment. Blood dripped from
her. "I'm hurt," she whispered over and over. She was rushed
to a hospital. An hour after her arrival she died. Redfern went
by bus to New York City and from there to Texas. After several
months he returned to his home town, the town in which Lizzie
Howard had lived. He hid in an old barn near his parents'
home. Within a week he was arrested. He had been traced to
New York, to Texas, and back to his home town. He confessed
readily, pleaded guilty, and was sentenced to life imprisonment
in the state prison without possibility of parole. That was eight
years ago.

Redfern's mother was interviewed, and I talked at length
with a man slightly older than Redfern who had known him
as a boy. Then I interviewed Redfern. The information provided
by the three people checked very closely. Therefore, I feel confident that in the following account of my interview with him

what Redfern says about his early life can for the great part be accepted as fact.

Arlin Redfern looked just about his twenty-six years. He was of medium height and weight, neat, had regular features. He was the kind of person about whom older people would have said, ten years ago, "he's a nice-looking, clean-cut boy." But now that clean-cutness was somewhat jaded.

I told him who I was, that I was doing research on why people get in serious trouble with the law. There was an ash tray on the table between us and he took out his cigarettes and lighter.

"Want one of these?" he asked me.

"No, thanks, I'll smoke one of my own."

He lighted my cigarette and then his with that kind of unnecessary, almost professional flourish that some people employ when using a cigarette lighter.

At this point, my main impression of Redfern was his array of small habits of speech and mannerisms designed to make others believe he was fully sure of himself. He was extreme in this. He swaggered when he walked, he spoke in a breezy fashion, he puffed on his cigarette with undue nonchalance. When I thanked him for the light, he said with a shrug of his shoulders, "That's okay, kid."

"The warden told me," I said to him, "that you don't particularly like working in the print shop."

He moved his shoulders and hands with that forced casualness. "It's all right with me. What difference does it make?" A brief laugh. "One place is as good as another here."

"Isn't there some one job you'd like to have?"

"I just told you. One's as good as another."

Four days ago Redfern had been released from light solitary confinement. He had been so confined—in an ordinary cell but away from all other inmates—for three months. During his eight years in prison he had been in trouble many times for violation of the prison regulations, unusual for a murderer.

"Why was it that you were in light solitary until the other day?" I asked him.

He had a way of laughing rather sarcastically while he talked. "Well, now, why should I tell you that? What's it——"

"Don't, then." Each person requires a different approach.

For a passing second he looked startled. "No, it was—I couldn't get along with a couple of those guys I was working with. I asked them," meaning the prison administrators, "to lock me up for a while." He had regained his nonchalance.

"Why did you ask to be put in solitary?" It was true that he had made this request.

"I told you, kid, I couldn't get along with a couple of those guys. Some of them, they bug me, I tell you. Don't do their work and it comes back on me. I was getting ready to let them have it. So I figured I better get out of there." He laughed. "I like it all right in solitary. Up there away from everybody, I kind of like it, off by myself."

"But you wanted to get out, didn't you?"

"Yeah. You get tired of it after a while, laying around there all the time. It begins to get you. No exercise, that's what it is. You get to aching all over."

"Do your relatives ever come to visit you?"

He laughed very abruptly. "Those bastards. You think they'd do anything for me? Listen, if they'd just do one thing, just one thing, I might feel different."

"But they do come to visit you?"

"Oh, yeah, sure. When it suits them. But they don't do a thing."

"It costs a lot of money, though——"

He grew excited. "Money? Money doesn't mean anything to me. To me, money's like the wind. I have it, it's gone. It comes again or it doesn't. What do I care?"

"No, I meant it costs a great deal of money for legal fees."

"I don't mean that. They've got no chance of getting me out of here. But if they'd do just one little thing, bring me something, send me something. But would they?" He laughed at the ridiculousness of it.

"You don't like any of your relatives?"

"Christ. Listen, when I was a kid I was their punching bag."

"How do you mean?"

"Beaten. Beaten all the time, kid. That's what I mean." He was laughing as he said it.

"For example?"

"For example? Listen. I had an uncle—I lived with him and my aunt a good deal of the time. He came in once, got mad at something, and threw me across the room. I landed against the stove."

"How old were you, then?"

"Five. Six."

"Did other people beat you?"

"Of course they did. Oh, I could tell you stories, kid." He seemed to have to laugh as he talked about this. "I could tell you stories for five, ten hours." He pointed a finger at me. "Listen, one time my two brothers, my two older brothers, were home with me. My mother'd gone out. She sold plants downtown, strawberry plants, stuff like that. Well, I was alone with them. One of them, Jim, told me to do something and I said I wouldn't do it. I wouldn't do it just because he told me. I had pride, even then.

" 'We'll take care of you,' he said to me, and he went outside while my other brother, Bob, he kept me from getting away. Jim came back with six or eight of these sapling branches. You know what they're like? They're kind of springy, and they split them up between them and began to beat me. They beat me for it must of been an hour. Anywhere they could hit me. They began to raise welts all over me. I could see them on my arms. Long swellings with the blood oozing through. Finally, I passed out and they must of kicked me under the bed because when I came to my mother was pulling me out from under the bed."

"What did she do?"

"Oh, she put stuff on me and put me to bed."

"Did she seem to feel badly about it?"

"Oh, kind of. But I don't know, she never seemed very sorry about anything like that."

"What did she do to your brothers?"

"Nothing. I didn't dare tell her. Because I knew they'd beat me again just as bad or worse. But then I went into what must of been a coma because my mother told me later I'd been out cold for two days except for when she first came home."

"Did other things like this happen to you?"

"Oh," he laughed, "I could go on like this for hours."

He had to laugh when he told about these things, because it hurt him so much to talk about them and yet he wanted to get them out of his system.

"Wasn't there a time when your uncle put you under the hood of a car?" I asked him.

He looked surprised but did not question how I knew. "Yeah, that bastard," he said seriously. Then he began to laugh as he talked. "Jesus, that was the same one, the same uncle I lived with for a while. He had this great big old touring car and he got the engine running and the side of the hood up. Then he shut off the engine and he grabbed me and stuck me in there and closed down the hood. I kicked and screamed because I couldn't get out. He started up the engine and there was a little light in there and I could see that fan whizzing around there. Of course, he shut off the engine after a while but I didn't know he would. I was just a little kid and it was the same the next time. He did it a couple of times. I was afraid I was going to die. And, you know, when he'd put me in he'd say, 'This time I'm going to leave you in for good.' But he'd let me out after a while and I'd see his big red face and he'd be laughing and I'd run and run."

"Why do you suppose your brothers and your uncle did these things?"

"I don't know. Just to be plain mean, I guess." He cocked his head. "I've tried to figure it out," he said, "and I think they did it because they were hurt themselves. We were all as poor as could be, we had nothing, and I think they tried to take it out on me because they were hurting so themselves. I think a lot of people do that."

"I agree with you."

"And—oh, Christ—there was another trick he pulled, this same uncle. He hooked up a wire or something to the car battery and then he had another end of it in a bucket of water and he got one of my brothers to get a third piece of the wire.

85

Then he got me out in the yard and he told me he wanted to give me some candy. Then my brother stuck the end of that wire to me from behind and, Jesus, I went up in the air. And then they laughed and laughed.

"You'd think a kid like me would know better but I was only five or six and I didn't understand it then."

"Was your uncle drinking when he did these things?"

"No, he didn't drink. My old man did. And my mother did. But not him."

"Did your mother or father beat you?"

"No, not much. I remember once my mother got mad at me for something and she grabbed a broom and began hitting me with it but it didn't hurt much." He was laughing again. "Then my father came in and he saw she wasn't really hurting me and he grabbed one of these towel racks from the wall. It was pretty thick wood and he began hitting me with that. I tried to get my head in the way because that way the stick might break. But it didn't break and after about three hits on the head I had to let him hit me all over. That was some beating."

"But usually your father didn't beat you?"

"No, he left me alone most of the time." He thought of something else and laughed sarcastically. "Oh, and then there was the time my brothers were going to teach me to swim. I couldn't of been more than four then. A ways from the house there was a river down a bank and they got me over there and I thought they were going to teach me in a little pool that was there. But they grabbed me and started swinging me and they threw me out in the river. The water was all around and I went downstream. I didn't know what was going on, I was half choking to death. And then I hit a rock and the next thing I knew I was up on the bank. I ran home as soon as I could, as soon as I stopped choking, but my brothers, they'd got there first."

"Was your mother there?"

"Yeah. They'd told her they were teaching me how to swim and even then I didn't dare say anything because I knew what would happen to me if I did."

"What did your mother say?"

"She just said how nice it was that I was learning to swim."

"Have you ever told anyone else about these things that happened to you, anyone here in the prison?"

"No." And now he wasn't laughing at all. "No, I've never told anybody. I think about them a lot sometimes but I never tell anybody anything like that." He grew superficially cocky again. "I don't tell anybody anything. I just act as if I'm making out all right."

"Can you think of other incidents, other things that happened to you?"

"I told you. I could keep you here all night." He paused and then he pointed a forefinger at me. "I'll tell you what I am afraid of. Snakes. I always have been and I'll admit it. I don't know why, I guess I was born that way. Now don't get me wrong. I'll fight one if I have to. I'll fight anything, anybody, if I have to. Somebody in here crosses me, I'll fight him. I don't care how big he is. I don't care what happens to me. I'll just give it every-thing I've got. I've been hurt and I don't care how much I get hurt."

He waved his hands, moved his shoulders, and laughed. "Well, that's something else, but what I was going to say is my two brothers knew I was afraid of snakes and they got hold of me. One of them had this snake, it must of been about three feet long, and they tied it," his voice rose, "they tied it around my neck. I tell you, I went out of my mind. I can't remember anything after that. I must of got it off after a while, I don't know. For almost a week I was half out of my mind. I didn't know what I was doing. My mother told me later. She was here a few months ago, before I went in solitary, and she mentioned it again. She said I'd been out of my head about a week."

"Did she seem to think it was a serious thing?"

"I don't know. She keeps saying how it's so odd I was always so afraid of snakes as to let it bother me. Listen, I'll tell you an-other thing. They all had this Christmas party—over at my uncle's. The whole family was there. They had presents for all the kids. And this uncle of mine, Harry, he asked me what I'd like most for Christmas. I said I didn't know, anything would be fine. I wasn't suspicious or anything. It was just that I was a little kid and, you know, you ask a kid what he wants and he doesn't exactly know. He's glad to have anything that's nice.

"Anyway, this uncle went out and he came back a little while later with a brown paper bag. They started handing out the presents and he gave me this bag. I looked in it. You know what was in it? Horseshit. He'd gone out there and got it off the manure pile in the barn."

"What did you do?"

"I went outside and I just dropped it over by the barn."

"Then what did you do?"

"They called to me and I went back to the door. They said they had a real present for me. It looked like a white handkerchief or something. I said, 'No, thanks. I don't want it.' I walked off and I went on home. It was snowing hard, I remember that." A pause. "Oh, well, the hell with it. The hell with them all. I go my way and they go theirs."

"But it all had a big effect on you, didn't it? All the beatings, all the meanness toward you when you were a child?"

Redfern shrugged. "Yeah, I suppose so. But, see, I never let them know it hurt me. I'd never do what they wanted. They wanted me to act like it hurt me but I wouldn't. Now I can take any kind of punishment. It doesn't matter what it is. Pain, it means nothing to me. I can kind of lay in it and know it's there and yet I'm kind of off somewhere looking on at the same time."

I would only talk with him this one time and there was no opportunity in the prison for any sustained psychiatric therapy. So I had to try to help him gain some insight into his own situation. But I was taking a chance because he might cut himself off from me.

"Look," I said to him, "I don't know whether this is correct or not—you know a lot more about your life and your situation than I do. But from what you've said and from what I know about you, it looks as if the way you were hurt as a child led you to get in the trouble you did. And now it's leading you to get in deeper and deeper here in prison."

He lit a cigarette with elaborate casualness. But he didn't cut himself off from me. "Maybe," he said.

"At the rate you're going you'll never get out of here. You'll——"

He laughed. "Listen, kid. When I came through those gates I said I was going to die in here."

"And you still think that?"

"Of course I do. I've got no chance."

"You keep thinking that and you won't have. There's such a thing as a self-fulfilling prophecy. You become convinced of something and you act in such a way that little by little you bring it about."

"So what am I going to do? I'm in for life, kid. And that's that." Then his eyes brightened. "I had an escape all rigged. Me and another guy. But they found out about it."

"How did they find out?"

"He told them. The other guy."

"Well, anyway, the point is, you're getting in deeper and deeper. I'm not talking about just the fact of your causing trouble in here. I'm talking about you. You're doomed, at the rate you're going."

"I told you, kid. I'm in for life."

"I know, but others who've been in for life have gotten conditional pardons. After eighteen or twenty years. That's a long time but it's better than not at all."

"With my record? Don't be silly. I haven't got a chance."

"I know, but if you were able to start out now and build up a good record, in about ten years you'd have a chance."

"No, no. Not me."

"What it amounts to is this," I said. "In one part of your mind, you don't want to get out. You were hurt so much as a child, you've gotten to the point where you like punishment."

"I like it?"

"Yes, you do."

He waited a moment. "Yeah, I suppose I do, in a way." He waved his hands. "No, no, I don't really like it. But I can take it if I have to."

"That's exactly what I mean. In a way you like it but deep down underneath you don't. It's just that you were hurt so much you've gotten used to it. In a way you feel comfortable getting yourself in a position where you'll be hurt because then you know where you stand."

"That's right," he said. "You know, that's right."

"If you're not being hurt you don't know what to expect."

"I know it. That's right."

"But at the same time you want to lead a decent life. You want to get out of here, settle down somewhere where it's quiet, get a job you like."

All his casualness was gone now. And what I was saying was hurting him, hurting him in a way that didn't give him a masochistic pleasure, because a decent life was what he really wanted. But I had to go on with it because someone had to try to light a positive spark in him.

"Wouldn't you like to have a boy of your own?"

"Of course I would. Ah, what's the use? All this doesn't mean anything. I'll never get out. It's impossible."

"It's possible."

He mustered his defenses. "You know, you guys bug me. Psychiatrists, psychologists, sociologists, all of you. You're the sociologist, that right? Yeah, well, anyway, you bug me. You tell me I ought to have hope. But you don't understand. You can't *feel* like I feel. I *know* it's no good to have hope. Something always comes along to louse things up."

"You know what the trouble is?"

"What?"

"You're so afraid of disappointment. You're afraid to take a chance by having hope, by trying to work for a pardon."

"Listen, I've always been disappointed. As a kid it was nothing but disappointment. You understand me, nothing. And since then it's been the same."

"But that doesn't mean it always will be."

He waved his hands and smiled. "No, I suppose not. But it does for me."

"You don't trust anyone, do you?"

"No, not a goddamned one. Trust? Jesus."

"Say you had a little boy. Would you trust him?"

"That would be different. Yeah, I'd trust him. Look, stop talking about this having a little boy, will you?"

90

"I'm trying to show you that it's possible to trust someone."

"Not me. I don't trust anybody. I tell you, you guys bug me. Coming in here and telling me what I ought to do. There's been three or four of you. I never liked any of them."

"How do you feel about me, right now?"

He thought about it. "To tell you the truth, I kind of like you. You can believe that or not."

"I believe it. But why? Why do you?"

"I don't know. You don't act like you know everything. I'll tell you this, you've gone a lot further, a lot deeper with me than any of the others. That stuff about liking to be hurt and being afraid of disappointment. It's true. Now, don't get me wrong. I don't *like* to be hurt. But the way you put it, knowing what to expect that way, it's true."

"As I told you, I'm talking about you. About what's going to happen to you. I don't care about what's easiest for the prison. I'm simply saying you've got to think about yourself in a sensible way, plan sensibly so you can get a pardon some day."

He cocked his head. "What are you spending your time with me like this for? What are you getting out of it? Doing this survey or whatever it is, I can see that. That's what you do for a living, I suppose. But the last while you've been talking about me. Telling me how I ought to plan for the future. What are you getting out of it? Why do you bother?"

"I suppose one reason is because I can see myself in your place—if I'd had the childhood you had. And then another reason is—well, sometimes you see someone like you, who is dragging himself down and down and you just plain want to try to help him. We all feel like that sometimes, that we just want to help someone."

He looked away embarrassed, and said, "Yeah, I knew. I could of figured it out. But I was just—I was just trying to be sure. I was just going back to my—to being like I usually am. Not trusting anybody."

Now he regained his composure again. "All right," he said, "suppose I did try to get along so I could get a pardon. Just what should I do? Tell me that, then, just exactly what should I do?"

"Well, I don't claim to know all the answers. I don't know the prison a hundredth as well as you do."

"That's for sure."

"But I'd say that first you should try to get a job here in the prison that you'd really like. Something where you had to figure things out, a job that made you think."

"How am I going to do that?"

"I don't know, figure out what you'd really like and ask the warden."

"Listen, I don't ask anybody for anything, not anything."

"What do you expect him to do? Read your mind?"

He smiled. "No." Then, "Oh, I asked for a job a while ago, in the woodworking shop. But do you think they'd give it to me? No."

"Did you really want it?"

That brief, startled look came over his face. "No, I didn't want it. I just thought I'd ask for it."

"But you can't ask for what you really want because you're afraid of being disappointed?"

"Yes, I suppose so."

"Is there any job here you really want?"

"Yes, there's one. But it's so—I'd never get it."

"Why?"

"They have to trust you."

"You mean it's outside the prison wall?"

"No, no. They have to trust you to do the job right."

"How do you know the warden wouldn't trust you?"

"He wouldn't. Not with my record."

"But, you see, you've got an answer for everything. An answer that makes anything you might try to do impossible. That way you don't have to take a chance and you won't be disappointed."

He nodded in agreement. Then he took another tack, trying to avoid the subject. "I will say this about the warden. He's been decent enough to me. He's a—a humanitarian. That may sound crazy coming from me but it's true. He does his best to help the men in here. And he's always been fair with me. He's never piled it on. Each time I get in trouble he acts like it's never happened before. Because of the other times, he could really pile it on, have me in solitary for a year. But he doesn't. And another thing. I remember once I got in trouble. It was a misunderstanding. The warden told me I could do something but he didn't tell the guard. So the guard pinched me. You know what the warden did? He admitted he'd been wrong himself. You've got to respect a man for that."

"That's why I say you ought to pick out a job you'd like, something you could really get interested in and ask him about it. But it ought to be a job where you wouldn't be working with too many people."

"That's right. That's what I'd like. Off by myself, working on something." He began to grow excited. "You know what I like?" he said. "Science. Anything like that. I was reading a book the other day. All about cockroaches. You wouldn't think that was much, would you? But it is. The way they breed, the way they eat and everything. It's—it's fascinating. Then I was reading another one. About wheat. The way wheat grows, from just a little seed. This book had pictures of the seed under the ground, growing. And then it took you through the whole thing, how the wheat was made into other things."

Redfern leaned back in his chair and put his hands behind his head. "I like all kinds of things like that. Stars. Astronomy. That really gets me. I've studied a lot about the stars. I can lay in my cell and look out through the bars and up at one star. Just one star. And I—I think about how far away it is and how it got there."

He laughed at himself in an open way, not sarcastically. "Ah, I'm crazy, I guess. Sometimes I lay there and I think about being in an airplane, flying up and up through the sky toward that star. All alone up there by myself, going through the night. Jesus, that would be something. I'm almost happy just thinking about it. But then I get this feeling and I say to myself, 'What have you got to be happy about?' and the feeling I had about being up there in the air is gone."

"Suppose you did get out of here eventually and could settle down somewhere. Do you think you could ever be happy or do you——"

93

"Of course I could."

"Some people can't, you know. Some people think they can but then when the time comes they really aren't able to."

"I could. I know I could."

"But the problem for you is getting some sensible plan, isn't it? So you can get a pardon eventually."

He was leaning on the table now and his hands moved so they were in front of his face as he answered, "Yes, sir." He was embarrassed to use the word, sir, and yet he wanted to. From kid to sir was a long way for him to have come in one afternoon.

"Besides changing jobs in prison," I said, "another thing you might try to do is study some one thing you're interested in. Go into it deeply, don't jump from one thing to another too much."

"What? Like the stars, like astronomy, or some kind of science?"

"Yes, figure out what you're most interested in. And try to study so that you could use it later. For example, you might study in such a way that you could get a job as a laboratory assistant."

"Nobody'd hire me." He grew defensively cocky, took a cigarette from my pack on the table. "Mind, kid? I like these. Good smoke."

"No, go ahead."

"Besides, where'd I get the books?"

"Get them from the library here. If the library doesn't have them, ask the education officer to send for them, borrow them from another library. That can be done."

"He'd want to know why I wanted them."

"Tell him."

He smiled knowingly. "He'd think I was trying to pull something. He doesn't like me."

"Look, don't you realize that you keep closing all the doors on yourself?"

"Yeah, you said that. Listen, I told you. You don't see my side of it. You don't know how I feel, how I can't ask for things like that."

"If we could know completely how other people feel, there might be no trouble in the world."

"You know, that's right. I've thought about that. But nobody can ever know how somebody else feels."

"No, but we can try."

"Yeah, I suppose."

"Have you read much psychology, sociology?"

"Yeah, some."

"You like it?"

"I liked it. All that stuff about why people do what they do. That fascinates me, too. Sometimes I try to just figure out why some guy acts the way he does, what makes him the way he is."

"Well, you might go into psychology and sociology deeply."

"They don't have the books."

"Talk to Morgan. You know him, don't you? Ask him about it." Morgan was an inmate who had studied psychology and sociology over the past ten years and had gained a great deal of knowledge of those fields. Now, he was being considered for a pardon.

"He'd want to know what I was up to."

"Is that so bad?"

He didn't answer.

"You like Morgan?" I asked him.

"He's all right. I'll say this for him. He's done something for himself here. He's really gone into that stuff—psychology ——" He paused. "But he's got it. He's an intelligent guy."

"You're as intelligent as he is, I'd say."

"Maybe." He tried not to show it but he was very pleased with the compliment.

"You see, if you got a different job here and if you studied something you liked, you might begin to get somewhere. And if you studied psychology and sociology, you'd gain a better understanding of yourself. We all need to do that, you know."

Redfern grew excited. "Look, I told you. I told you. I'm not asking for anything."

"I'm not trying to be unsympathetic but——"

He interrupted me, waving his arms, more excited. "I don't want sympathy from anybody, you understand me? Nobody. I don't expect sympathy from anybody. I don't want it."

"Don't you think it's rather odd that you get so emotional about the word, sympathy?"

His excitement came to an abrupt halt. "Maybe. Maybe it is."

"I simply meant that I didn't want to seem as if I were passing off lightly the fact that you've got to spend ten years or more in prison even if you do try to be constructive."

"I know."

It was time for the interview to come to a close. I said to him, "And about this matter of not being able to leave yourself wide open to disappointment by trying anything constructive or asking for anything. You don't have to leave yourself wide open. You can just think about this for a while. Think sensibly about what job you might do best at here. Study a little bit. Talk to people about these things just a little. Don't be so extreme in your thinking. Be somewhat flexible. You can open yourself to the world just a small amount. Leave the door open just a little at times and see what happens. You can't be very disappointed that way. And if everything goes all right, then you can open the door a little more."

He had been listening intently. He shrugged now, not in his cocky way but rather as if to say: maybe. It was better than if he had said he couldn't do it.

I got up to leave and he walked down the barred corridor with me to the control room. I had moved much too fast with him, of course. But it did not seem likely that I would see him again. So I had no choice. Still, I thought I had reached him.

We stopped at the door which was electrically operated from the control room.

"About the being flexible, I see what you mean," he said. He put out his hand and said, "Thanks."

"Thank you for talking with me."

Then the door swung open and Redfern walked away, down the corridor leading to the cells. I watched his walk grow nonchalant and cocky. He was putting on his psychological armor.

This is a case where physical frustration and psychological frustration in early life are exemplified. Apart from the frustrations Arlin Redfern mentioned, his leg was pierced by a home-made javelin when he was about eight years old. I believe one of his brothers threw it, but I have not been able to ascertain for certain whether it was a brother or someone else. And when Redfern was three months old, he had a series of convulsive seizures. His mother thought he was going to die. A doctor was called, but I do not know how serious the doctor thought the situation was. As far as is known, the convulsions did not return.

Redfern has been diagnosed psychiatrically as a borderline psychotic with strong paranoid traits. In the above record of my interview with him, one can see glimmers of his paranoia. Certainly this paranoid strain is readily understandable. He was hurt so much that he became, in effect, simply overly suspicious of everyone and everything.

As is also clear from the interview, Redfern has developed a masochistic approach to the world. No one, I think, fundamentally welcomes pain and punishment. But the basic drive to avoid pain can become overlaid with its opposite. As in Redfern's case, the welcoming of pain serves to provide a feeling of security, serves to obviate the advent of a more cruel possibility: disappointment. I mean disappointment due to the actions of one's fellow human beings. And after all, other people are all we really have in this world. Also, of course, masochism tends to reduce guilt, if only temporarily.

As a juvenile, Redfern carried out a number of thefts and he frequently fought with others. These were both attempts to release aggression and attempts to seek punishment. But they were not enough to quell the complex mixture of aggression feelings and guilt within him. When Lizzie Howard attempted to prevent him from stealing from her, the aggression poured out of him.

Perhaps Lizzie Howard, middle-aged, represented his mother to him. His mother was in a sense certainly at the center of his frustrating world when he was a child. She could have protected him but she did not. However, I am leary of attaching too much significance to these possible symbolic representations. They may have validity and they may not. One never really knows, not even after prolonged psychiatric probing.

In any event, when Redfern attacked Lizzie Howard, his tremendous pent-up aggression found an escape valve. And at the same time, he purposely laid himself open to frustration.

He fled but he returned, thus really insuring capture and imprisonment. And he thereby insured also that punishment would partially expiate his guilt feelings. Further, he insured a psychological return to his painful childhood. Terrible as our childhoods may have been in some cases, we want in one part of our beings to reproduce them. It was then that we were almost totally dependent on others for our existence. Frustrating as those childhoods were for men like Redfern, they represented living rather than dying. And so there is a certain drive for security in the attempt to return to them.

Since I interviewed him, I have thought many times about Arlin Redfern. I have thought about what might have been if, when he was a child, his relatives had been educated to realize consciously the motivations that led them to aggress against him. I have thought of what might have been if he had received psychiatric treatment in adolescence. I have thought what might be if he were to receive psychiatric treatment even at this late date. And, finally, I have thought, as I have in the cases of many other murderers, that there but for the grace of environmental circumstance go I.

4. Psychological Frustration

THE fifty-one men convicted of murder apparently experienced psychological frustrations which were significantly greater in number and intensity than those experienced by their control brothers. These psychological frustrations arose largely from the following: physical defects which were, in effect, social stigmas; overly rigid, inconsistent, and emotional behavior by the parents, especially the mothers; severely frightening experiences of a definitely traumatic nature; and lack of acceptance, approval, and prestige in school and community. Battered by physical frustrations, the murderers were further beset by psychological frustrations which swelled their reservoirs of aggression to a point where that aggression eventually would, and finally did, burst its confines violently.

Ten of the murderers and two of the brothers were reported by the mothers to have been born with some extreme, severe, visible physical defect. None was born with more than one such defect. These defects were of the type that would be likely to cause others to react negatively, that might well cause the individual social embarrassment in childhood, adolescence, and adulthood.

The preponderance of such defects in the murderer group as compared to the brothers is statistically significant at the five per cent level. (Using a two-by-two table, $X^2 = 6.046$) One murderer was born with an abnormally large head; a second with a club foot; several with eyes which were, and appeared to other individuals to be, abnormal. Still another was born with a badly twisted neck, and so on.

The mother of a boy who at nineteen had killed a near stranger after an argument said to me, "I don't know that it had anything to do with the trouble he got in, but he was always so sensitive like about that neck. He thought people was looking at him. I used to tell him, 'Now, nobody's thinking anything about it,' but he had it in his head that they was always looking at him."

Visible physical defects of an extreme nature which occurred *after* birth were over three times as prevalent among the murderers as among the control brothers. Specifically, these defects were present in the cases of sixteen murderers and of five brothers. ($X^2 = 7.256$; $P < 0.01$; two-by-two table used.) No individual had more than one such defect.

These, too, were the kinds of defects which are likely to cause embarrassment in social situations: facial scars, crippled legs and arms, and the like. And that embarrassment can be considered a frustration factor.

Many murderers do not, of course, have any such defects. Still, it is important to note that among the fifty-one murderers there was a total of twenty-six instances of extreme visible physical defects (those which were present at birth combined with those which developed later); among the fifty-one control brothers there was a total of only seven defects. Thus, there were almost four times as many visible defects among the murderers as among the brothers, according to the mothers' statements. It may be that in the cases of the defects which occurred after birth the murderers tended, more often than the brothers, to become involved in situations, such as fights and accidents, where they were likely to be disfigured. Nevertheless, the defects, once existent, can reasonably be assumed to have led to psychological frustration.

Consider now the parents' actions toward the murderers and control brothers. To what extent did the parents cause psychological frustration in their sons? On the basis that a mother's behavior toward a newborn child is likely to be influenced by whether she wished to give birth, the mothers were asked, "How happy or unhappy were you when you found out that you were going to have the child?" The mothers' answers distributed themselves in the way shown in Table 1.

Table 1

Mothers' Attitudes toward Prospective Births of Murderers and Control Brothers

	Number of Murderers	Number of Brothers
Very Happy	19	23
Somewhat Happy	7	11
Neutral	9	12
Somewhat Unhappy	9	2
Very Unhappy	5	2
Don't Know	2	1
Total	51	51

Of course, the mothers' answers may have been distorted. They may not have wanted to admit they had been unhappy about giving birth. Also, knowing now that one son was a murderer, they may have remembered their feelings prior to his birth as more negative than they were at the time. None the less, fourteen of the mothers said they had been somewhat or very unhappy about the prospect of the murderers' births while only four said they had felt that way about the coming of the control brothers' births.

In interviewing the mothers, I had the distinct feeling that in actuality they had resented the births of the murderers more frequently than those of the brothers. In some cases, the mother was not married when she became pregnant; in others, she had too many children to handle as it was; in still other cases, she was not well and pregnancy was an added burden. Here are statements by two mothers which bear on this point:

"Well, the truth is, me and my husband wasn't married then—when I found out I was going to have him. He did the right thing, I'll say that. We was married right away. But I was afraid somebody'd find out. It was a terrible time."

A trim little woman who had had ten children, one of whom had strangled to death a young girl, said: "I tell you, I had eight of them running around. I was run ragged and I come to find out I was going to have another. This is too much, I said to myself, but what could I do? He came, all right. And what happened? The worst thing that could. He went out and—and—" The mother could not bring herself to say that her son had committed murder.

The mothers were also asked whether they were "getting along" with their husbands "very well," "moderately well," or "poorly" when their sons were born. The responses indicated no real differences in cases of the murderers as compared with the control brothers. Fifteen of the mothers said they were "getting along poorly" when the murderer sons were born, and fifteen said they were "getting along poorly" when the brothers were born.

As I have mentioned previously, the parents seldom separated or divorced. But in a fair number of cases they were clearly very unhappy living together. However, even where there was a wide difference in the ages of the murderers and control brothers, the parents were on the whole probably as unhappy during the infancies and childhoods of the brothers as of the murderers. The main point here is that in about a third of the families, very likely more, the murderers developed in an atmosphere of severe parental discord which was largely kept hidden from public view.

I would characterize the mothers' approach to the murderers, during infancy and childhood, as one of doing generally what appeared to be the accepted thing and of mixing with this a great deal of disguised aggression. According to this view, the mother's aggression could have caused frustration and hence aggression in the child. There appears to me to have been an interplay of aggression and frustration between mother and son with the father somewhat indirectly involved.

The interplay seems to have proceeded frequently in this fashion: the child had been frustrated physically through illness or other factors discussed in Chapter 3. This made the child aggressive, especially difficult. The mother, frustrated because of her low station in life and high expectations, directed her aggression against the difficult child, the murderer-to-be. He became all the more aggressive although not necessarily in obvious, direct ways. The mother, upset and exasperated, occasionally directed her aggression toward the father as well. He retaliated toward her and sometimes toward the child. To the father, the child seemed to be the root of the trouble.

According to the mothers, they tended rather equally to be solicitous of the murderers' and control brothers' needs during infancy. When asked the question, "What did you usually do when the child cried during his first year of life?" the mothers responded in this way:

	Number of Murderers	Number of Brothers
Went to Child Immediately	27	27
Waited 5 or 10 Minutes, Then Went to Child	15	19
Let Child "Cry It Out"	8	5
Other	1	0
Total	51	51

There was a definite tendency for the mothers to feel that they had pampered their children during the first year of life. But the possibility that they actually did so is not borne out by answers to other questions. For example, the schedules the mothers followed when caring for the infants were rather rigid, just slightly more so for the murderers than for their brothers.

The mothers were asked, "How rigid were you in trying to keep to a definite time schedule while caring for the child during the first two years of his life?" In a majority of cases of both murderers and control brothers, the mothers said that they were very rigid or moderately rigid:

	Number of Murderers	Number of Brothers
Very Rigid	18	15
Moderately Rigid	13	12
Moderately Flexible	13	19
Very Flexible	7	5
Total	51	51

Again, when asked the more specific question, "During the first two months of the child's life, did you feed him on a fixed schedule, on demand, or on a combination of the two?" the mothers' replies indicated that they were slightly more rigid with the murderers than the control brothers. Here is the distribution of responses:

	Number of Murderers	Number of Brothers
Fixed Schedule	28	20
Demand Schedule	11	15
Combination	11	14
Don't Know	1	2
Total	51	51

Going by the mothers' reports, thirty of the murderers and twenty-five of the control brothers were bottle-fed during the first two months of life. Conversely, seventeen of the murderers and twenty-four of the brothers were breast-fed. The remaining four murderers and two brothers were both breast- and bottle-fed. Bottle-feeding is probably less rewarding than breast-feeding. But, the differences in numbers of murderers and brothers so fed are not large enough to warrant attaching any extreme importance to them. However, I was struck by the fact that many of the mothers appeared to have guilt feelings about not having breast-fed their children—murderers and control brothers alike:

"I tried but I couldn't. I should of, I guess. But it wouldn't work and I had to give it up."

"The milk was—what you call sour. I had to use the bottle. What else could I do?"

I asked this mother, "Do you think feeding a baby from the breast is better than from the bottle?"

"That's what I'm saying. But like I told you. The milk was what you call sour. I *had* to use the bottle."

There were no real differences in the ages of the murderers and the control brothers when the mothers started weaning from the breast or bottle. Early weaning can be considered a frustrating experience, and I had thought the murderers might have been weaned relatively early but this was not the case. Six to eleven months was the most common time for weaning both murderers and brothers from the breast. And twelve to seventeen months was the most common time for weaning murderers and brothers from the bottle.

Abrupt weaning, as distinguished from early weaning, can also be considered frustrating for the child. Therefore, this matter was investigated. Here, again, there were no real differences between murderers and control brothers. Of the twenty-one murderers and twenty-six brothers weaned from the breast, a decided majority of each were weaned in a month or less. Of the forty-one murderers and thirty-five brothers weaned from the bottle, a majority of each were weaned completely in three months or less, usually less.

While no important differences were found between murderers and brothers with respect to weaning, there were significant differences as to ages at which the mothers began toilet training. On the average, the mothers said they started to toilet train the murderers at an earlier age than they did the brothers. In the cases of twenty-nine murderers and eighteen brothers, toilet training was begun before age one year. On the other hand, in the cases of twenty-one murderers and thirty-two brothers, this training was begun after age one. Information was not available for one murderer and one brother. (See Table 8, Appendix A, for details and chi-square figure.)

Why, on the average, did the mothers begin to toilet train the murderers earlier than the control brothers? I suspect that the mothers were more aggressive toward the infant murderers-to-be than toward the brothers. And the early toilet training was one indirect way in which the mothers could unconsciously vent their aggression while rationalizing their actions in the name of cleanliness. As previously mentioned, it appears that because of early illnesses the murderers were greater problems to the mothers than were the control brothers. And if the mothers unconsciously resented the potential murderers for being problems, the mothers' consequent actions only served to increase the magnitude of the frustration.

The average person finds it next to impossible to accept the idea that if toilet training is begun early and is forced, it is severely frustrating for the child. He either passes it off as of no consequence or half-jokingly says, in effect, "Sometimes you psychologists and sociologists talk as if you think everything a person does depends on toilet training."

Toilet training is neither of no consequence nor does it in itself determine completely any later behavioral form. But if a mother is not basically affectionate toward the child and if she forces him too fast in this regard, he will be greatly strained to meet her demands. He is likely in later life to be especially anxious about defecation matters and to have a vague but deep-seated feeling of deprivation.

The time required for the mothers to effect the toilet training of the murderers and brothers was also investigated. The differences between the two groups were not large. Nevertheless, the nature of the small differences found is of some importance. The time required to toilet train the murderers tended to be slightly extreme—shorter or longer than to train the brothers. Of the seventeen children trained in one month or less, ten were murderers. And of the fifteen children where training took longer than one year, ten were murderers. This is a pattern that will be evidenced with respect to certain other spheres of behavior: the training of the murderers and their actual behavior were more extreme, tended toward both ends of a given continuum to a greater degree than was the case with the control brothers.

Turning to the matter of sexual training by the mothers, it is clear that as a group the mothers were strongly repressed about sex. They attempted to strait-jacket their children, both the potential murderers and the control brothers, with respect to sex. They succeeded in making the children unduly curious about sex yet guilty when they attempted to satisfy that curiosity. And guilt feelings are frustrating.

The mothers were questioned concerning the extent to which they explained sexual matters to the murderers and brothers when they were about six years old. Forty-nine of the fifty-one mothers said they had explained nothing about sex to the children. The remaining two mothers had explained about sex to a small extent. While the mothers were usually not explicitly asked whether their husbands had explained sexual matters to the children, I gained the distinct impression that the husbands almost invariably did not do so. Discussion of sex was tabooed in the great majority of these families. Here are conversations with two mothers which bear on this point:

Interviewer: "When the boy was around six years old, did you ever explain to him about sex?"

Mother: "No. Well, maybe I should have. Or my husband, maybe he should have. But we just—we just didn't talk about things like that. Certainly not to the children. Why, my husband and me, we never talked about things like that between ourselves. We, oh (brief laugh)—we had the children, of course. We were man and wife, I mean to say. But we never talked about it."

Another mother said, "No, it's not good to tell children those kinds of things. They find out enough, out on the streets, believe me, without being told at home."

"Do you think that sexual relationships outside of marriage are ever all right, under any circumstances?" I asked her.

"No, I don't. Don't believe in it. I never have."

"I don't mean as a general thing. I mean in rare cases where——"

"No cases. It's a sin before God. A sin before God."

"Do you mind my asking you these questions about sexual matters?"

"Well, no. You're supposed to be one of those psychiatrists or so-chiatrists, aren't you? Ask away. I'll say what I said, it's a sin before God."

"How did you feel about your boy getting in the trouble he did?" Her son, at eighteen, had raped and then beaten to death a middle-aged woman.

"How did I feel? I couldn't believe it. But he must of done it. He said he did."

"Do you have any idea why he did it?"

"Well, she was leading him on, from what I heard. But that wasn't all of it."

"What was the rest of it?"

"Bad blood, that was the rest of it. In spite of all I did to try to make him a good boy. It was his grandfather—his great-grandfather, his father's grandfather. He's got that blood in him. That's where it come from."

The mothers were all asked the question mentioned in the conversation above: "Do you think that sexual relationships outside of marriage are ever all right, under any circumstances?" Forty-eight of the mothers said that such relationships were never all right, were always bad. One said they were all right, not bad, under exceptional circumstances. The remaining two mothers were undecided, said they did not know. Given the fact that the forty-eight mothers who answered negatively might have been attempting to impress the interviewers with their morality,

108

their answers still have considerable importance in that they indicate a part of the face the mothers show the world with regard to sex.

The mothers were asked if they had ever made the murderers and control brothers stop sexual self-play and, if so, how old the sons were when they first stopped them. Twenty-nine of the mothers said they had never stopped the murderer sons, and thirty said they had never stopped the control brothers. Most of these mothers claimed that, to the best of their knowledge, these sons had never as children indulged in sexual self-play. Practically all children do engage in this self-play, but many of the mothers apparently had chosen to ignore the matter.

Table 2
Ages of Murderers and Control Brothers When Mothers First Stopped Sons' Sexual Self-play

	Number of Murderers	Number of Brothers
3 Months or Less	0	1
Over 3 Months to 6 Months	2	0
Over 6 Months to 1 Year	8	4
Over 1 Year to 2 Years	5	8
Over 2 Years to 3 Years	2	5
Over 3 Years to 4 Years	1	1
Over 4 Years	2	1
Age Unknown	2	1
Doesn't Apply *	29	30
Total	51	51

* Mothers did not stop sons' self-play.

It is interesting to note in Table 2 that of the fifteen children whom the mothers said they stopped from engaging in sexual self-play during the first year of life, ten, or two-thirds, were murderers-to-be. On the other hand, of the twenty-five children whom the mothers said they stopped after the first year, fifteen, or three-fifths, were control brothers.

The mothers were also asked to what degree, if any, they were emotionally upset the first time they observed the murderers and control brothers in sexual self-play, regardless of whether they stopped them. Again, there are no important differences when the mothers' reported reactions to the murderers and to the control brothers are compared. However, of the mothers who admitted that they had observed either the murderers or the brothers or both in sexual self-play, a great majority said that they were "very upset" rather than "somewhat upset" or "not at all upset."

With respect to their feelings about their sons' sexual self-play, here is what two fairly typical mothers had to say:

"I didn't know what to do. A little thing like that—playing with himself. Well, after all, I was afraid he might keep on doing it, when he grew up, if you understand me."

"I was so upset I had to lay down. I didn't know anything about those things, then. I came from people where those things were never mentioned. Never. I was just nineteen or twenty at the time. After I'd had the other kids I begin to see it was what they all do but I didn't know that, not then."

The mothers were questioned concerning the worst type of behavior manifested by the murderers and control brothers at age five. The answers distributed themselves as shown in the table on page 111.

As is evident, in the cases of the mothers who answered the question, sexual self-play was far and away considered the worst type of act committed by either the murderers or the brothers. The mothers' most usual action when confronted by this sexual self-play was to emotionalize—cry or scream—and sometimes to hit the child as well.

The mothers were asked whether the murderers and control brothers had been sexually attacked during the first twelve years of life. The mothers said that to the best of their knowledge three of the fifty-one murderers and none of the brothers had been so attacked. The difference in numbers is too small to allow the drawing of any conclusions. But it is noteworthy that with respect to this and other types of situations mentioned in this chapter which might reasonably be presumed to give rise to frustration, the differences while small are almost always in such a direction that they indicate greater frustration for the murderer group than for the control group.

	Number of Murderers	Number of Brothers
Sexual Self-play	15	13
"Talking Back" to Mothers	4	4
Fighting	2	4
Stealing	1	0
Lying	0	1
No opinion	29	29
Total	51	51

The question of how many murderers and brothers were as children severely frightened by other individuals, but not sexually attacked, was also investigated. The mothers said that during the first twelve years of life seven murderers and two brothers had been severely frightened once or more by some individual.

Further, the matter of whether the murderers and brothers were severely frightened by some natural event during their first twelve years was examined. According to the mothers, six of the fifty-one murderers and four of the fifty-one brothers were frightened in this way. These natural events were fires, lightning, falling rocks, and the like. Here, too, the difference is very small. But again it is in a direction which is indicative of greater frustration for the murderer group than for the control group.

We are not concerned in this chapter with the mothers' and fathers' training per se of the murderers and brothers. But we are concerned with the possible psychological frustration that the training might have caused in the children. Therefore, it will be well to consider the extents to which the mothers became angry at the children, cried, isolated themselves from the children, and were inconsistent in carrying out expected punishments and rewards. Table 3 presents this information as provided by the mothers.

Table 3

*Frequency of Selected Responses by Mothers toward Murderers and Control Brothers during First 5 Years of Life **

	Anger		Cried		Isolated Self	
	M	B	M	B	M	B
Very Often	12	9	10	3	5	1
Occasionally	18	25	8	18	9	7
Seldom	20	17	33	30	37	43
Unknown	1	0	0	0	0	0
Total	51	51	51	51	51	51

	No Threatened Punishment **		No Promised Reward **	
	M	B	M	B
Very Often	6	4	1	1
Occasionally	21	21	18	17
Seldom	24	26	31	33
Unknown	0	0	1	0
Total	51	51	51	51

* "M" designates number of cases of murderers. "B" designates number of cases of control brothers.
** Mothers threatened punishment, or promised reward, and then did not carry out the threat or promise.

With the exception of the responses for "no promised reward," the "very often" frequency occurs more among the murderers than among the control brothers. If one takes all five types of responses and summates the number of cases of murderers where the response was "very often," a total of thirty-four is obtained. And if one does the same for the control brothers, a total of eighteen is obtained. Thus, these five types of responses were directed "very often" at almost twice as many murderers as control brothers. And these types of responses I consider to be ones which will cause anxiety and frustration in a child.

The mothers' responses of "cried" and "isolated self" were "very often" directed at the murderers in an especially larger number of cases than they were at the brothers. Crying and self-isolation when young children do things of which the mothers disapprove are, I am convinced, very frustrating for the children. In almost any family, the mother is the symbol of the sources of life to the child. Even if she has not been a particularly attentive mother, she has nevertheless very likely supplied the children with food, warmth, clean or at least dry clothes, and some affection.

A professional thief, who had killed during a holdup but who was not a professional murderer, told me, "Whenever I did anything wrong as a kid, my mother would get very upset and cry. She'd cry and cry and she'd go to her room and lock the door but I could still hear her crying. It made me feel awful. I knew I'd done something but a lot of the time I didn't know what and she wouldn't tell me. She'd just cry."

He was a very intelligent man with a great deal of personal insight. "When I was fifteen or sixteen, I began running around, getting in a lot of trouble. I'm not blaming mother for anything, but sometimes I honestly think I did some of those things just to hurt her for having hurt me. I knew if she found out what I was doing she'd cry, but I didn't care any more if she did."

Another man serving a life sentence for murder told me, "Anything we kids did wrong, she'd go in her room and stay there for three or four hours. Then when she'd come out she wouldn't talk to us for maybe half a day. And it happened more with me than the other kids. I always seemed to be getting in more trouble—at least doing things my mother didn't like. The thing was, she didn't seem to tell us beforehand what we shouldn't do."

Why did the mothers tend to cry and isolate themselves more with respect to the murderers than the control brothers? First, I interpret crying and isolation of this nature to have been veiled acts of aggression on the mothers' parts. Unconsciously, at least, they knew these actions would hurt the children. Second, and as hypothesized earlier, the mothers were perhaps more prone to hurt the murderers than the brothers because, generally, the murderers had been greater problems to them.

The mothers tended to be quite strict with their sons, although not in a consistent fashion. When asked the question, "Were you very strict, moderately strict, or not at all strict in training the child when he was about five years old?" the mothers replied as follows:

	Number of Murderers	Number of Brothers
Very Strict	25	21
Moderately Strict	18	21
Not at All Strict	7	9
Unknown	1	0
Total	51	51

The mothers were also asked, "Do you think mothers of today pamper their children too much?" Thirty-one mothers said, in effect, "Yes, definitely." Seven answered, "No," and the remaining thirteen said they did not know.

At the same time, the mothers had, I felt, guilt feelings about their strictness toward their children, especially toward their murderer sons. Going on the assumption that the mothers' guilt feelings would be partially reflected by their responses, they were asked, "How often were you afraid the child would get hurt when he was about five years old?"

Regardless of how frequently the mothers *actually* were afraid their sons would be hurt when about age five, a distinctly larger number of mothers said they were frequently afraid in the cases of the murderers than in the cases of the control brothers. Twenty-four mothers responded that they were "almost always" or "usually" afraid with respect to the murderers, while only eleven said this with respect to the control brothers. (See Table 9, Appendix A, for the full distribution of responses.)

Learning the use of language is a behavioral area in which the murderers experienced a considerable amount of frustration. The mothers reported that, as a group, the murderers first spoke intelligible words at a later age than the control brothers:

Age in Months	Number of Murderers	Number of Brothers
Under 18	15	27
18–29 *	34	22
30 or Over *	1	1
Never *	1	1
Total	51	51
$X^2 = 5.828$		$P < 0.05$

* Combined for X^2 calculation.

There is, then, a significant difference, as reported by the mothers, in the ages at which the two groups began to speak. How does one explain this? I think the most likely explanation is that the murderers, having experienced more frustration than the control brothers during the first year of life, were somewhat blocked by anxiety. At the same time, slowness in learning to speak is, I think, frustrating in itself. The child cannot communicate his needs as well without language as with it. Therefore, his needs tend, to some extent, to go unsatisfied. Further, parents are apt to be upset with a child who is slow in learning to speak and this causes him added frustration.

This phenomenon has arisen at least implicitly in preceding

pages: frustration tends to beget frustration. An individual who has been severely frustrated is unduly anxious and therefore cannot learn as efficiently as he otherwise would. This makes those around him impatient, exasperated with him. They react negatively toward him, thereby increasing his frustration. He responds by some manner of aggression. In the case of slow speech learning by the murderers, I think there was this added element of aggression. The child senses that the parents want him to speak and he aggresses toward them, frustrates them, by slow learning.

This process of frustration begetting frustration seems to be an especially dominant theme in the development of the murderers. It can even grow to the point where the individual seeks frustration. He has learned to expect it and in a certain sense he feels comfortable with it. Quite clearly, that is what happened in the previously presented case of Arlin Redfern.

About one-fifth of the murderers and of the control brothers, ten murderers and eleven brothers, learned some other language before they learned English. Eventually they all learned English with the exception of one murderer and one brother who were mutes. Learning one language, then learning another which is to become the major tongue, can be construed as frustrating for young children. This is not to say that learning English first, in our society, then learning at ten or eleven a foreign language, to be used as a secondary tongue, is anxiety provoking. But to learn a foreign language at home, then to enter the first grade and be forced to learn English quickly, is frustrating. And that is what most of the ten murderers and eleven brothers were forced to do. They were expected to speak English at school, the parent tongue at home. Conflict, anxiety, and frustration can be assumed to have been the result. Further, the interviews indicated that they experienced embarrassment in school because of their lack of facility with English. James La Casse is an example here. Of course, this embarrassment was as true for the control brothers as a group as for the murderers. Nevertheless, it is one more indication of the climate of frustration in which some of the murderers developed.

Learning to read is another important area of language behavior. Here is the way the murderers and control brothers were distributed with respect to the general difficulty they had in learning to read, as judged by the mothers:

	Number of Murderers	Number of Brothers
Almost No Difficulty	24	34
Moderate Difficulty	16	14
Great Difficulty *	9	2
Never Learned *	2	1
Total	51	51

$$X^2 = 6.430 \qquad P < 0.05$$

* Combined for X^2 calculation.

To a significant degree, the mothers reported that the murderer group had greater difficulty learning to read than did the control group. Here is another foundation stone for the theses that murderers have experienced more frustration than nonmurderers and that frustration begets frustration. The murderers were generally highly frustrated when they first went to school. Their resultant aggression brought more frustration upon them. Probably, their anxiety and repressed aggression tended to retard their reading. And this brought on still further frustration.

By and large, the murderers did poorly in school, did not like it, and left as soon as they could, thus virtually precluding any possibility of entering a prestigeful, satisfying occupation. Quite clearly, judging by the mothers' responses to questioning, a distinctly larger proportion of the murderers than of the control brothers disliked grammar school. Of the murderers, twenty-three were reported to have liked the first four years of grammar school, and twenty-three were said to have disliked school during that period. (Five were considered to have been neutral.) On the other hand, the mothers reported that, of the control brothers, thirty-seven liked school while only five did not. (Nine were neutral.) These differences are statistically significant at the one per cent level. (Table 10 Appendix A.)

A number of behavioral forms which are driven by anxiety and frustration were investigated as to whether they were manifested by the murderers and control brothers during their preadult years. They would serve, as it were, as partial indices of the degree of frustration experienced by the individuals in the two groups. Examples of the behavioral forms are phobias, compulsions, stuttering, and the like. Naturally, in questioning the mothers, it was made clear in everyday terms what is, for example, the actual nature of a compulsion.

Table 4 indicates that seven of these behavioral forms—phobias, compulsions, obsessions, bedwetting, stuttering, sleepwalking, nightmares—were said by the mothers to have been manifested by a greater number of murderers than of brothers during the preadult years. With respect to presence and absence of five of these forms of behavior—all except obsessions and stuttering—the differences between the murderer and control brother groups were significant at the one or five per cent levels.

Phobias, compulsions, and obsessions have much in common. Not only are they indicative of earlier frustration per se, but also there is generally a guilt component in each of the three behavioral forms. Further, they are ways of trying to handle repressed aggression. It is striking that the mothers reported thirty-four instances of phobias, compulsions, and obsessions for the murderer group and only three instances for the control brother group. It is highly unlikely that this vast difference can be accounted for on the basis that the mothers gave distorted answers to questioning.

A considerably larger number of murderers than brothers were said to have been persistent bedwetters or stutterers. These are two types of behavior that not only imply earlier frustration but that when manifested are fairly likely to beget frustration. Both bedwetting and stuttering are socially embarrassing in our society.

Most of the cases of stuttering occurred around ages six or seven and were severe for a year or two. In most instances the stuttering was almost unnoticeable as the children moved into adolescence. However, the stuttering pattern tended to return during adulthood, the mothers said, when the sons were in stress situations. And this was especially true of the murderers.

Table 4
Presence or Absence of Selected Behavioral Forms Indicative of Frustration during the Preadult Years of Murderers and Control Brothers *

	Phobias		Compulsions		Obsessions		Persistent Bedwetting	
	P	A	P	A	P	A	P	A
Murderers	17	34	13	38	4	47	18	33
Brothers	2	49	1	50	0	51	3	48
	$X^2 = 14.552$		$X^2 = 11.922$				$X^2 = 13.492$	
	$P < 0.01$		$P < 0.01$				$P < 0.01$	

	Stuttering		Persistent Sleepwalking		Persistent Nightmares	
	P	A	P	A	P	A
Murderers	10	41	8	43	11	40
Brothers	5	46	2	49	3	48
	$X^2 = 1.954$		$X^2 = 3.992$		$X^2 = 5.300$	
	$P > 0.05$		$P < 0.05$		$P < 0.05$	

* "P" indicates presence of behavioral form.
"A" indicates absence of behavioral form.

During the interviews with the mothers, questions were asked concerning how frequently the murderers and control brothers had become emotionally upset at about age five, excluding anger and temper tantrums. To a highly significant extent, the murderers as a group became upset more frequently than did the brothers. (Consult Table 11 in Appendix A.) Twenty of the murderers were said to have become emotionally upset once a week or more, but none of the brothers were said to have done so this frequently. Here is another piece of evidence to bolster the view that because of early frustration the murderers were as children less emotionally stable than the control brothers.

A further point: according to the mothers, the murderers were, as a group, more solitary in childhood than were the brothers. When asked whether their sons spent a majority of their playing time alone or with other individuals at about age five, the mothers reported as follows:

	Number of Murderers	Number of Brothers
Alone	12	2
With Other Individuals	38	48
Unknown *	1	1
Total	$\overline{51}$	$\overline{51}$

$$X^2 = 8.304 \qquad P < 0.01$$

* Not included in X^2 calculation.

The whole lower-class situation in which most of the murderers were immersed by circumstances of birth was a broad frustration factor in itself. True, it was equally so for the control brothers. But they had generally not been subjected to the extreme amounts of other frustrations that the murderers had. It is the totality of frustration we are concerned with here. To use an analogy: when you are carrying a hundred pounds on your back for a long distance, the addition of an extra ten pounds seems like a much much greater extra burden than does the same ten pounds if you have been carrying only twenty.

It is true that some individuals seem content with lower-class status and probably do not experience anxiety because of it. By and large, however, the murderers' and control brothers' parents were, in my judgment, people dissatisfied with their lot in the prestige hierarchy of the society, people with strong drives to rise in the social class system. These drives were usually frustrated but they were there. The murderers, and probably the control brothers, had similarly strong upward mobility strivings which were thwarted. The overwhelming majority of murderers with whom I have talked or whose biographies I have read have seemed to me extremely sensitive about their lack of social class prestige.

Related to this is how the murderers and control brothers felt about their occupations. The mothers were asked to judge how well the murderers liked their work just prior to the murders. In the cases of the brothers, the mothers were asked how well they liked their work when they were at ages equivalent to the murderers' ages just prior to the murders. Here are the mothers' judgments concerning how well their sons liked their work:

	Number of Murderers	Number of Brothers
Very Much *	10	21
Considerably *	4	12
Somewhat **	7	6
Not at All **	14	1
Unknown ***	5	2
Doesn't Apply ***	11	9
Total	51	51
$X^2 = 19.006$		$P < 0.01$

* Combined for X^2 calculation. ** Combined for X^2 calculation.
*** Not included in X^2 calculation.

There was, then, a tremendous difference in how well the two groups liked their work, if one accepts the mothers' judgments as being valid. It is reasonable to assume that those who do not like their work are frustrated by it and by their general social situation. Again and again I found murderers who said they had had absolutely no interest in the occupation in which they were engaged just before they committed murder.

An Index of Psychological Frustration was constructed in much the same fashion as was the Index of Physical Frustration. One point was given the individual for the known presence in his preadult experience of each instance of fifteen selected types of psychological frustration. For example, one point was allotted for each trauma due to natural events or other individuals which occurred before the age of twelve years, physical beatings excluded. (See "The Index of Psychological Frustration," Appendix B, for the full list of fifteen factors.) The minimum possible score on this index was zero while there was no limit as to the maximum.

The scores for the murderer group were significantly greater than for the control brother group. Ten murderers had scores of two or less while twenty-eight brothers had these scores. On the other hand, the scores of nineteen murderers were six or higher, but only three brothers had scores at that level. The mean score for murderers was 4.7; for the brothers the mean score was 2.5. (Consult Table 12 in Appendix A for the full distribution of scores and for the chi-square figure.)

The scores were also analyzed with respect to the differences within pairs of murders and control brothers. It was found that in thirty-four of the fifty-one pairs the murderers had higher scores than the brothers. In ten pairs, the scores were equal. And in the remaining seven pairs, the brothers had higher scores than the murderers; the difference here was usually one point.

The Index of Physical Frustration and the Index of Psychological Frustration were combined to provide an Index of General Frustration. The score for a given individual on this Index of General Frustration was found simply by totaling his scores on the physical frustration and on the psychological frustration indices. Here, seventeen murderers had scores of five or less on the Index of General Frustration as compared to thirty-six control brothers. At the other extreme, nineteen murderers had scores of eleven or higher while not one of the brothers had a score above ten. (See Table 13, Appendix A.) To the extent that the mothers' responses reflected the facts, here is great weight in favor of considering frustration as a possible major influence behind murder.

The mean score for the murderers was 9.24; for the brothers this score was 4.20. Comparing scores within pairs of murderers and control brothers, it was found that in forty-two pairs the murderer had a higher score than his brother. In five pairs the scores were equal. And in four pairs the brother's score was greater than the murderer's. That is to say, 82 per cent of the time, forty-two out of fifty-one, the scores agreed with the basic idea stated in the central hypothesis of the study: that the preadult frustration of murderers is greater than the preadult frustration of nonmurderers.

The Case of Henry Savoy

HENRY SAVOY is a slim, seemingly quiet young man, twenty-six years old. He has rather sensitive, regular features, is fairly good-looking without being startlingly handsome.

Here, pieced together from conversations with him, is Henry Savoy's story, in his own words:

My folks were both French. I mean they came from French people way back. When I was born in 1931 they had the ground floor in a three-family house. It was on the bank of a river and in the summer there used to be floods and sometimes my folks had to move out for a couple of weeks till the water went down.

The first thing I can remember was when we had one of those floods. After it started to go down there was a kind of lake left behind the house, and I remember paddling around on it on a kind of raft. I must of been about three and a half. I remember just paddling around there and having fun. I don't know why but that's the first thing I remember.

My father ran a machine in the mill where they made shoes. He got paid pretty good, nothing great but enough so we always had everything we needed.

The thing about my mother was, she was such a strong Catholic. She got awful upset if anybody didn't go to church. Both her and my father were pretty quiet generally. I had a sister two years younger than me and a brother eight years younger. Whenever one of us kids would do something wrong, my mother would get pretty upset and cry and tell us how bad we were. Then when my father came home from the mill, she'd tell him what we'd done and he'd tell us how bad we were.

They never hit us but I didn't like being told I was bad and I'd get awful mad. I'd go into my room and feel bad about it and then feel mad. I wouldn't do anything about it and the next day I'd probably forget about it. That's the thing about me. I get mad quick and I get over it pretty quick.

No, my mother usually didn't tell us ahead of time not to do something, but then if we'd do something wrong she'd get upset and cry, like I say. But she was awful strict about church things, like not stealing, and sex, and things like that.

When I was five they sent me to the Catholic school. The sisters there were awful strict. I got along all right the first little while, but then after I'd been there about two weeks this nun hit me. We'd been out playing in the yard—during recess—and when we went in she came up to me and said, "Why were you doing that out there?"

I didn't know what she meant and I said I wasn't doing anything. She was just a little pip-squeak, only about four and a half feet tall, but she looked big to me then and when I said I wasn't doing anything she bashed me alongside the head.

I got mad and I took out of there and kept on going till I got home. I told my mother what happened and the next day my mother went down to the school and told them they'd better leave me alone. I never did know what I was supposed to have did wrong when the nun bashed me.

A couple of days later I went back to school. The second day I was back a nun yelled at me and I began to get mad and then I blacked out, fainted. The next thing I knew I was home in bed. The doctor said I had a nervous breakdown so the rest of that year I didn't go back to school.

The next year I started in the public school. I liked that better. They weren't so strict. But I never liked schoolwork much. I never liked learning things. Now, I wish I'd done different in school but I didn't like it much then.

I got on all right, though. I passed every grade but I was always near the bottom of the class. I got along pretty good with the other kids. I always had somebody to play with, anyway.

There were these two brothers, the O'Hara brothers. I used to play with them a lot. They were older than me and bigger. But they were in the same grade as me so they must of been pretty dumb. We used to get in fights a lot. They'd do something I didn't like or I'd do something they didn't like and I'd lose my temper and see red and sail right in. I didn't care who it was, when I got mad I'd start fighting. Sometimes I'd win and sometimes I'd get a black eye. If I'd get a black eye, my mother would start to cry and tell me I was bad and then I'd get mad again.

I remember when I was about nine or ten, my father had an old rowboat and he'd let me take it out on a little bay like in the river. He'd fixed up an old engine for the boat and it would go along pretty good. This one day I got out in the bay and the engine stopped. I wrapped the rope around the thing—the rope you're supposed to start it with—but it wouldn't start.

I got mad and I wanted to do something so I pulled that engine off the back of the boat and threw it in the bay. Then I rowed back to the shore as fast as I could. I ran to the shed and got a hammer. I began beating on the boat, trying to knock it apart, and about that time my father came along. He stopped me and he was pretty mad, mostly about losing the engine, but he didn't hit me.

I remember another thing that made me awful mad. I had this little brown dog, and him and me used to go everywheres together. Well, one day him and me went running out of the house, and the dog got in front of me and I tripped over him and fell. I got myself skinned up pretty bad. I was blood all over. I went back in the house crying and my mother saw what had happened and she started to cry and get mad. She got awful upset. She wanted to kill the dog. She claimed it was all the dog's fault that I'd gotten skinned up. I got mad about that because it wasn't really the dog's fault, but she was blaming him anyway. But then in a couple of days I forgot about it.

When I was about eleven years old they put me in a Catholic school again. I went into the fifth grade but the Catholic school was ahead of the public school I'd been going to so they made me stay back a grade. I didn't like that and after that I never did any homework. My mother used to ask me if I didn't have homework to do and I'd tell her I just didn't have any. They were awful strict in that Catholic school and I didn't like it.

I'd go out playing with the O'Hara kids and then about this time I got to know this other kid, Herby. And he and me became best friends. We used to go everywheres together. I never got in any fights with him like I did the other kids. We got mad at each other once. We were building this tree house, up in a tree down by the river. I wanted to put it up high and he wanted it down low, so we got mad at each other and we stood there getting ready to fight. But then we both turned around at the same time and walked away and went home. The next day we were good friends again. He was about the only one that I couldn't hit. With any other kids if I got mad I'd just kind of go out of my head and start swinging.

The only time I ever did anything really wrong was this time Herby and me went down to this big garage and started throwing rocks through the windows. We were just doing it to have something to do. But this man drove up in a car and he almost caught us. After that I never did anything like that again.

When I was fifteen I started in the Catholic High School. I wanted to play football and I went out for the freshman team. I was doing pretty good but they had this coach, and he told me that when I got to be a senior I wouldn't be able to play football because I'd be nineteen years old and that was too old. I couldn't understand that, but that's what he said. I guess it was politics mixed up in it. Anyhow I couldn't see much point in going to high school if I couldn't play football on the varsity. I didn't want to do any studying. So I went home and told my mother and father I wanted to quit. They got awful upset about this, but finally I talked them into it. I told them I wanted to go to work. So they let me quit.

I got this job working in a bakery and restaurant. I was a dishwasher. But I didn't like the work and after two weeks I quit. What I didn't like was the boss, the guy who owned the place. He kept piling extra work onto me and I didn't get any more money for it so I quit. Then a little while later I got a job in a restaurant across town. First they had me making the coffee. Then they put me on to making sandwiches and then after a couple of months I began to learn to be a short-order cook. And that's what I did there after that. That was a good job.

My father had a 1946 Plymouth, and he used to let me use it while he was at work. He worked the two to eleven shift at the mill and I worked the night shift at the restaurant. So at two o'clock I'd go down to the mill with him and I'd take the car and I'd have it until eleven when I'd pick him up. I got running around with a couple of guys and we used to go out drinking beer—not a lot, maybe three or four beers each. We never did much of anything else. I liked mainly just to drive the car. I like cars and I like driving.

This one time we were driving around and one of these fellows knew some girls that were walking up the street. So we stopped the car and got to talking to them. Then they crowded in and we went driving around. That's how I got to know this Barbara that I went with before I went in the Navy. She and me went together for three or four months. She was a Catholic and pretty strict and she didn't like the idea of my drinking beer. I got to drinking a little more and now and then I'd get drunk. One time I went to her house when I was drunk and she said she wouldn't have anything to do with me after that. And that's when we broke off. I never had much to do with her as far as sex goes because she was too strict about things like that.

Then a while later I met this Peg. She was just the opposite of Barbara. She liked to drink better than anything. She and me got going together. About that time I got in this argument with my father over the car. I wanted the car this one night and he said I couldn't have it, but he wouldn't tell me why. I got mad and that afternoon I went down to the Navy place and filled out the papers for enlisting in the Navy. I was only seventeen and I still had to get my father's permission. So that night I took the papers home and showed them to him. And I showed them to my mother too. My mother started to cry right off and went into her room. My father sent me into my room and then he went and talked to my mother.

A little while later he came into my room and he walked up to me with his fist doubled up. "That was a crazy thing for you to do," he said. "But now that you've done it we'll have to go through with it." So he told me to meet him the next morning and we'd go down to the Navy place and he'd sign the papers.

The next morning we went down and he signed me in. He didn't say anything all the way down and back. But I think my mother must have told him it was all right to let me go in the Navy or he would never have done it.

Anyhow, a couple of weeks later I left for boot camp. I didn't like it there at all. Being told what to do all the time and marching everywhere, I didn't like that. But I didn't say anything and I got through all right. Then they assigned me to this ship that was in dry dock. And I was on that in the harbor for a couple of months. I liked it a lot better being on a ship. Then we went overseas for six months. We were in the Mediterranean and I liked that too. I always liked the sea, since I was a little kid.

When we came back I got a leave and I saw this Peg again. We drank together a lot and had sex together and then I had to go back to the ship. I was afraid she was pregnant so I went A.W.O.L. and went back to her. I spent six days with her trying to get her to go to a doctor. Finally she went to some doctor and I went back to the ship. I got ten days in the brig and a thirty dollar fine. They could of given me a lot more but the petty officer liked me and they let me off easy.

It turned out that Peg was pregnant but she knew a nurse that worked in this hospital and the nurse got her some kind of pills. The pills did the trick and she didn't have the baby.

A couple of months later I went A.W.O.L. again so that I could see Peg. I asked them for a leave first but they wouldn't give it to me so I just took off. I figured if I only got ten days the first time and thirty dollars fine that that was all they'd give me the second time.

So I took off and went home to my folks. They thought I was on leave. I was seeing Peg every day and then the shore patrol picked me up in town and took me back to the ship. This time they gave me three and a half months in the prison.

I got mad over the idea of them giving me only ten days the first time and then three and a half months the second time. So as soon as I got a chance before they put me in prison, I took off again. I went A.W.O.L. and I lit out for the west. In Ohio I ran into this girl and started living with her. She was pretty rich. I told her I had to go back and let my folks know where I was and then I'd come back to her, so she gave me the money for a round-trip bus ticket. I went back east to see my folks. I suppose

I should have just telephoned but, anyway, I went back. And while I was there the shore patrol came and picked me up again.

This time I got sentenced to six months more. So then they put me in the naval prison for nine and a half months. I got along there all right, all in all. I got mad at having to do what they said but there was nothing I could do about it. I only got in trouble once. I talked this guy in the tailor shop into putting some of these old zippers together and sewing this long zipper on my blouse. I didn't like the idea of having to pull the blouse up over my head every time I wanted to take it off. It made me mad so I had this zipper put on. I liked it because it was something a little different too. But the officer saw it and made me take it off and then I had to go before a board and they said I was defacing government property. I wasn't defacing any property, I was just putting a zipper on the blouse. I told them that but they gave me five days in solitary.

Just before I was to get out of prison I decided that I wanted to stay in the Navy. I was supposed to get a discharge with bad conduct. I didn't like the Navy much before but now I got to thinking that I'd like to stay in, so I told the Navy board this. But they said they didn't want anybody who had gone over the hill three times, there must be something wrong with him. I wrote my parents and told them to see what they could do about getting me to stay in. They got in touch with this congressman and he wrote a letter to the C.O. in the Navy prison.

The C.O. called me in and showed me the letter. "So you've got political influence, have you?" he said.

"I don't know anything about it," I told him. "I just wrote my parents asking them to see if they could help me."

The C.O. said that he'd already told me they didn't want me in the Navy, and I said I knew that but I thought I'd try to stay in anyway.

"You're one of those wise bastards, aren't you," he said to me. "Well, we'll fix you." And then they put me in the hole for ten days.

Just before I was to get out of prison I wrote my father and asked him if he'd try to pick me up a car for about a hundred dollars. When I got out and went home he had the car there for me. For the next three months I just stayed around home. I didn't do anything. I didn't feel like doing anything. I'd just fool around in the yard with the car. I didn't even get it registered for three months.

Then after three months I got a job as a short-order cook in a restaurant. I got the car registered and I began going out and drinking beer, going around with the guys. It was about this time that I met my wife, Pauline. One of these guys I used to go around with said he knew this girl over the state line who was pretty nice. So we drove up there one night. She was living with her parents but they were out. She came out in the car and we went driving. This night I didn't have my car. We were with this friend of mine. Pauline sat in the back with me and we got along good right off. I whispered to her that I'd tell the guy driving that I had to go back home for something, that I'd forgotten something, and then when we got to my house she should go and jump in my car and I'd get the keys and we'd take off.

So I got him to drive me home and then she jumped in my car and we took off. The other guys were kind of mad but there wasn't anything they could do about it. Pauline and me went together steady after that. We got along fine. We used to go to a show every night and things like that.

At first I thought her parents liked me all right. But then one night she and I were out driving and we ended up in the woods. I ran out of gas. So we stayed there all night. The next morning I got a milk truck to push me and I took her home. I wanted to explain to her father but he slammed the door in my face. After that her parents hardly ever spoke to me. A couple of weeks later I got to talk to her father and I told him that I'd never touched her and I hadn't. But he still was kind of mean about it and that made me mad.

Anyhow, that September, about six months after I'd met Pauline, we decided to get married. We made out an application and the next day my mother saw it in the newspaper and started crying and said how I should have told her first. Well, I told her then and she said we'd have to get married in the Catholic church. I said that was all right with me.

I went to see the priest and he said it would be a couple of months before we could get married because Pauline would have to be taught the ways of our religion. I told him we were going to get married right away. He said we couldn't and I started to walk out. Then he called me back and he said he'd write the archbishop to see if he could get a special case made of it. The archbishop wrote right back and said we could get married in two weeks if Pauline would study every day. So she went every afternoon and studied about the religion and then we got married in the church. Her parents were so mad they wouldn't even come to the wedding.

Pauline's father was a mechanic in this plant and he made pretty good money but they were awful stingy and never spent any of it. Why, lots of times after we were married I used to take Pauline places and buy her things and she acted just like a little kid because her parents had never bought her anything.

We got this apartment in her home town and I got another job as a short-order cook. Her parents would never come to visit when I was around. The only time they'd come was on Friday nights because I worked Friday nights.

Pauline had this old uncle. He was about seventy. He was supposed to have a lot of money and he lived by himself in a big old house. Outside it looked nice but inside it was about a hundred years behind the times. The old guy liked Pauline a lot and he used to give her five dollars now and then. It was just after we were married, he asked us what we wanted for a wedding present. I knew that he was supposed to have a lot of money so I said we'd like a car.

"What kind of car?" he asked me, and I said, "Oh, a new Ford or Chevrolet would be all right."

That kind of hit him but he said, "How much would that be?" and I told him, "Oh, about twenty-five hundred dollars, I guess."

The old guy said he'd see about it. Well, we used to go to see him about once a week because he'd always liked Pauline. But each time we'd go he wouldn't say anything about the car. After a couple of months Pauline asked him about it. He said his money was all tied up in bonds or something and he couldn't get it for us right then but he would later. We knew he was faking and we knew we'd never get the car and that made me mad, the old bastard. Telling us that he'd get us a new car and then not doing it. And the thing I wanted most was a new car.

Pauline and me first thought about it about a month before it happened. We were driving home and I said to her, "Suppose we were to knock out the old boy—your uncle—and take his money. What do you think?"

And Pauline said, "It would be all right. If we could get away with it."

Then the next day we kind of forgot it and nothing came of it.

The next time I thought of it was this night after we'd been to the show—the open-air theater. I'd been out of work for a month and I'd spent my last dollar to go to the show. I like movies and I'd spend my last cent on them. We drove out of the open-air theater and driving along the road I thought of it again and I said to Pauline, "He's supposed to have all that money. Let's go and knock him out and get it."

Pauline said it was all right with her and I drove over there to his place. I stopped for this red light and—I don't know—something happened. I kind of blacked out. The light changed three times and then Pauline shook me and said, "What's the matter? The lights changed a couple of times."

I started up the car and drove along in a kind of daze. I came to this intersection where you're supposed to turn right to get to his place but I went straight.

"You missed the turn," Pauline said, and I turned around and went back and this time I took the right turn. I pulled up in front of his place. It was about midnight and there was no lights on in the house. We got out and went up the steps and rang the buzzer. I rang three or four times but he didn't come. He was sleeping, I guess. So we went back down the steps and started for the car and then this cop came along. "What's going on?" he said, and I told him we were trying to make a phone call, there was something wrong with the car. So he left and just as we were about to get in the car I looked up at the house. There was this glass door and through it I could see a flashlight coming down the stairs.

"There he is," I said to Pauline and I didn't know whether to go back to the house or get in the car but then we went back up the steps and he opened the door and peered out at us.

Pauline said hello to him and he asked us to come in. She told him we had car trouble and he started into the living room. Just as he got through the door I hit him over the head with the pipe —I hit him hard enough to kill a bull—and he went down but then he started to get up again and I hit him a few more times. I got kind of mad, I guess, because he didn't stay down the first time. They said at the trial that I hit him a lot of times. I don't know. I guess maybe I had in the back of my mind about how he'd fooled us about getting us a car—telling us he'd get us one and then not doing it. I'm not sure.

Anyway, I told Pauline to wait in the hall and I went up the stairs to his bedroom and found the old trunk where he was supposed to have his money. Her parents, Pauline's parents, had always been saying that he was supposed to have four or five grand in there. The damn thing was locked and I couldn't get it open. I took the pipe and beat on the lock. I got it open and there wasn't a thing in it—nothing but a couple of old rags.

God, I was mad, after her parents always talking about how much money he had in there.

I went back downstairs and went through his pockets. He had a thirty-eight revolver in one pocket. I took it. See, if I hadn't hit him again after he went down the first time and then started to get up, he'd probably have used that gun on me. All the money I found was a couple of bucks in one of his pockets but what I didn't know was that he had two pair of pants on and in the inside pair he had about four hundred dollars.

Then we left and got in the car and started home. I didn't think he was dead but I knew we had to get out of town because he might bring charges against us. I didn't think he would because he always liked Pauline but I figured he might so we had to get out. We got some things from our place but we didn't have any money except the few dollars I'd taken from the old man. So we went over to the house of this friend of mine and I woke him up—it was about two o'clock in the morning—and told him I was in trouble and would he lend me ten dollars without asking any questions.

He gave it to me and we took off. We drove over into New York and then kept on going and we got to Jamestown and stopped there. I didn't have but only a couple of bucks but we got a place to stay in this woman's house for only a dollar a night.

I looked around for a job the next day but I couldn't find anything. I told this woman who owned the house where we were staying that we were broke and could we stay a few days and then pay her when I got a job. She said it was all right. She was nice to us. The next day I got a job in a restaurant working in the kitchen.

I watched the papers every day and listened to the radio but there wasn't a thing about the old fellow being knocked out. So I figured it had all blown over and I wasn't much worried.

I went on working at the restaurant and we were doing all right. We'd go to the show mostly in the evenings and I figured maybe after a while we could save some money and get a new car. Pauline seemed kind of happy, not doing much, just reading magazines during the day. Then we'd go out to eat and to a show at night.

And then the twenty-fourth day after I started working at the restaurant these two men came in and went over and talked to the boss. I heard them ask for me. I was cutting up vegetables but I had a cigarette going and then they called me over and I said, "Just a minute till I get these cut up."

I thought they were food inspectors and they'd give me a hard time for smoking around the food and I wanted to get rid of the cigarette. But they told me to come right over and they were police and they arrested me. They asked me where Pauline was. I told them because I knew if I didn't they'd find her anyway.

They took me down to the police station and I wrote out a statement saying that I'd hit the old man over the head. I didn't say I killed him because I didn't think I had. They brought Pauline into the station and they told her to write out a statement. I told her not to write anything and they told me to keep my mouth shut. Then they took her in another room and showed her my statement and she wrote out the same thing and signed. She always did just what I did. That made me mad, that they got her to write out a statement, because if she hadn't of, she'd be free, walking the streets today. Because the cop in front of the old man's house, he walked back later, while we were in the house, I guess. Anyway, at the trial he said he'd seen a woman in the car. And I would of said she was out in the car and didn't know what I was doing in the house. But—she signed the statement.

The police sent us back to stand trial. The state gave us a lawyer—a young guy just out of school, I guess—and he told us to plead guilty, that we'd get off easier. We did and that's where I made my mistake. I should of pleaded innocent. I think we'd have got off lighter. But I didn't know that then. So we both got life.

Now they say Pauline wants to divorce me. I don't understand. I still love her, as much as I ever did, and I know she loves me. I'd like to find what's behind it—why she's divorcing me. It's her parents, I know that, but I'd just like to find out for sure. They've been seeing her there in the prison and I can't get to see her. They've put the idea of divorcing me into her head. She doesn't think for herself and she'll listen to what anybody tells her.

Maybe if we didn't get divorced, maybe we could both get pardoned some time.

Before the trial the doctors—psychiatrists, I guess—gave me those tests. They said there was nothing wrong with me, that I was pretty smart and that I wasn't crazy or anything like that. I don't know. I know I'm not crazy but I couldn't have been very smart to do a thing like that—hit the old guy over the head so many times and then not even get any money. You've got to be pretty dumb to do that.

I've been getting along pretty well here in the prison. At first I was awful nervous, jumpy. But I've kind of got settled down and everything goes along all right. I'm the vegetable cook in the kitchen. Pretty soon I'm going to be the head cook and that's quite a lot of responsibility.

I've never broken any rules here. I've always got along all right. I play on the basketball team. We play outside teams. I do pretty well but last night I only got two baskets.

I like to go to the shows when they have them here. I like westerns most. I read some of the books in the library. I like sea stories best. I always liked to read about the sea. Some of the guys in here do handicrafts, make things and sell them, but I don't. I haven't got the patience for that.

Sometimes I get mad at—oh, little things that come up. If anybody blames me for something I didn't do, things like that. But when I get mad I keep it to myself. I don't do anything. It wouldn't pay in here.

Henry Savoy's mother was quite willing to talk with me. She said she had always been "high-strung," grew upset easily. She seemed to me to have a great deal of repressed aggression, to be prudish about sexual matters, to be overly concerned about what others thought of her, but to have a sense of humor. Judging from her statements, Henry's father was a passive man.

Mrs. Savoy said that Henry had had many fainting spells as a child, usually when something upset him. She reported that twice, at ages six and sixteen, Henry had lost his sight for a few days at a time.

Mrs. Savoy readily admitted that she cried a great deal when Henry was a boy, that she grew upset with him frequently, that she isolated herself from him occasionally.

Henry's mother started toilet training him at nine months. It took two to three years to complete the training. When he was a young child she stopped him from carrying on sexual self-play a number of times. She had been, she said, extremely upset about these incidents. She was never able to explain anything about sex to Henry.

Mrs. Savoy said that Henry had been extremely clean as a boy, bathed several times a day at different periods in childhood and adolescence, and combed his hair with great frequency.

As can be seen, there are several parallels between Henry's case and the case of James La Casse. Both are of French descent. Both mothers were much the same: easily upset, generally repressed, greatly concerned about others' evaluations of them. Apparently both fathers were quite passive.

Both Henry Savoy and James La Casse manifested periodic outbursts of aggressive behavior during childhood and adolescence. Each seems to have been compulsive, although this is not as clear in Savoy's as in La Casse's case. Each suffered a considerable amount of psychological frustration although La Casse was subjected to more purely physical frustration than was Savoy.

The superficial factor that triggered off Henry Savoy's aggression toward his wife's uncle was the uncle's promise of a new car and his failure to fulfill that promise. Henry put great value on a new car and felt extreme frustration at having the possibility of owning one dangled before him and then withdrawn. Also, Henry was aggressive toward the uncle for seeming to possess what was to Henry a large sum of money.

That Henry had at least unconscious plans to kill the old man is somewhat evident from the fact that when Henry and Pauline were driving to the uncle's house on the night of the murder, Henry went momentarily blank at the stop light, then missed the turn. He was, as it were, unconsciously trying to avoid the act which he felt driven to commit. When he did strike the old man with the pipe, he went much further than was necessary simply to knock him out.

Psychological tests given him just prior to the trial indicated that he has an over-all I.Q. of 109. Projective tests reflected, as is usual with murderers, emotional immaturity and lack of judgment. But they showed no extreme patterns of personality maladjustment, no evidence of a psychosis.

A glaring aspect of Henry Savoy's approach to the world around him is his reaction to frustration. Whenever frustrated, he seems to have shown a pattern of sudden anger, followed, when he considered it feasible, by outward aggression and rebellion. As a small child, he became angry when his mother criticized him, but he felt he could do nothing about it. When he grew angry at other children, he usually lashed out at them physically. When the engine of his father's boat frustrated him, he threw it in the bay. And when he was an adolescent and his father frustrated him by refusing him the use of the car, he struck back by applying for duty with the Navy. He went A.W.O.L. three times, apparently as a form of rebellion. (It is interesting to note that each time he so acted it was exceedingly easy to apprehend him.) Then, when he was being forced out of the Navy, he attempted to rebel again by changing his mind, wanting to remain in the service. It would seem that this pattern of aggressive rebellion was an outgrowth of extreme frustration, in good part at the hands of his mother, plus a lack of training in how to handle frustration.

Henry Savoy seems to have been trapped in a web of early psychological frustration, high moralizing, and little guidance. His main method of reacting to this was to rebel aggressively. Viewed in this way, it is understandable that he eventually killed someone whom he felt was frustrating him.

5. Aggression Release

THE fifty-one murderers appear to have released aggression during childhood and adolescence to about the same extent as the control brothers. However, the murderers tended to release their aggression in different ways than did their brothers. Broadly speaking, the murderers used channels for release which are probably somewhat unacceptable to the society at large while the brothers employed more acceptable channels.

Information was gained from the mothers concerning sixteen ways in which the murderers and the brothers could have released aggression in childhood and adolescence. I classified these ways into two groups: socially acceptable and socially unacceptable. The classification was based on my judgment as to whether the types of aggression release matched or did not match the prevailing values of the over-all culture of the total society. There were nine acceptable ways and seven unacceptable ways. The acceptable were: (1) general verbal loudness at age five; (2) anger short of temper tantrums at age five; (3) releasing anger verbally at age five; (4) physical fighting at age five; (5) "talking back" to the mother at age five; (6) dirtying clothes when "dressed up" at age five; (7) participating in athletics at age seventeen; (8) hunting at age seventeen; (9) mildly antagonizing others by verbal means at age seventeen.

The seven unacceptable ways of releasing aggression were:

(1) lying to the mother at age five; (2) stealing at age five; (3) swearing at age five; (4) temper tantrums during childhood; (5) severely hurting animals in childhood or adolescence; (6) fist fighting at age seventeen; (7) violent aggression other than fist fighting, when intoxicated, before the age of twenty. The various specified ages were used in order to allow for meaningful comparisons of the mothers' answers.

Someone else might classify these types of aggression differently than I have. For example, "talking back" to the mother could be considered unacceptable, and temper tantrums could be considered acceptable. However, there is no especially practical, objective way of making the classication. One can simply disagree with my classification if he wishes.

Consider first the acceptable channels of release. General verbal loudness, not directly connected with expressing anger, was not a way of working off aggression which was used by many of the fifty-one murderers. According to the mothers the murderers were as children of age five on the average much more quiet than their brothers, although the latter were not unduly loud:

	Number of Murderers	Number of Brothers
Loud *	3	3
Average *	14	35
Quiet	34	13
Total	51	51
$X^2 = 17.400$		$P < 0.01$

* Combined for X^2 calculation.

As can be seen, over two and a half times as many murderers as brothers were considered quiet by the mothers; while two and a half times as many brothers as murderers were considered average in regard to verbal loudness. Frequently the mothers indicated to me how quiet the murderers had been when young:

"He was awful quiet as kids go. I don't know why it was. He was always like that. He'd get mad, all right, but the rest of the time he was so quiet."

"I used to think there was something wrong with him, he was that quiet. He'd go for hours without saying a word, except 'Yes' and 'No' as you'd ask him."

"Well, Harry was quiet and he wasn't. What I mean is, he was quiet to the extreme but then all of a sudden he'd start yelling about something. That's the way he went—quiet, then yelling, but mostly quiet."

While they were generally quiet, the murderers were said by the mothers to have grown angry short of temper tantrums more frequently at about age five than did the brothers. There were twenty-nine murderers and twenty-nine brothers whom the mothers reported grew angry at about age five. Of these, sixteen murderers and two brothers grew angry very frequently, once a week or more often. Here is an instance where the murderers chose an acceptable aggression outlet to a significantly greater degree than the brothers:

	Number of Murderers	Number of Brothers
Once a Week or More	16	2
Less Than Once a Week (But at Least Once a Month)	10	12
Less Than Once a Month (But at Least Once)	3	15
Never	22	22
Total	51	51
$X^2 = 19.070$		$P < 0.01$

The mother of a man who went berserk, killed a friend with a knife, said, "Oh, but he'd get mad when he was a little kid. He wouldn't say much but he'd get so mad you'd of thought he was going to bust. And just a little thing four, five years old."

"How often did he get mad?" I asked her.

"Oh, a lot of the time. Every few days, it seemed like."

"Well, would you say once every two or three days, once a week, once every two weeks?"

"Oh, sometimes more, sometimes not, but I'd say about once a week. Oh, but he'd get mad."

Another mother said of her son, a boy who at seventeen had had sexual relations with a girl, then beaten her to death: "He was always so quiet. No, he never got what you'd call angry. I never knew if he did, anyway. He'd get to feeling bad, a lot, feeling kind of sad, I'd call it."

"At what times would he do that?"

"Well, when something would go wrong in school or playing with the others, something like that."

"But he never got angry when he was about five?"

"No, not as I knew. Just feeling bad a lot."

Showing anger is in itself a way of dispelling aggressive feelings. However, there is also the matter of whether acceptable verbal channels are used to reduce the anger once it has arisen. Anger when one is frustrated and aggressive, is, up to a point, adjustable; an acceptable way of ventilating that anger, such as accusing others in a fairly reasonable way, is also adjustable. But here the murderers reversed themselves, as it were. That is, as a group they grew angry more often than the brothers but they much less often used acceptable verbal channels to reduce the anger. Unacceptable channels, verbal or otherwise, such as persistent screaming or kicking, do not concern us at this point. They will be considered later when we deal with temper tantrums.

Of the twenty-nine murderers and twenty-nine brothers who were said by the mothers to have grown angry at age five, almost four times as many brothers as murderers, fifteen to four, released anger in a reasonable verbal manner to a great extent, i.e., "usually." Three times as many brothers as murderers, nine to three, released anger in this way to a moderate extent—"about half the time." On the other hand, over four times as many murderers as brothers, twenty-two to five, "seldom or never" employed this verbal channel. (See Table 14, Appendix A, for the chi-square figure.) Why did the murderers not use this channel? This is part of a larger question: why do murderers tend to be overconforming most of the time and violent occasionally? I shall try to answer this toward the end of the chapter.

When they were about age five, the murderers fought physically with other children to a markedly lesser extent than did the brothers, the mothers said. Again, I would consider fighting at this age to be fairly acceptable behavior from the point of view of the total society although some mothers would violently disagree with me.

Approximately the same numbers of murderers and brothers, twenty-two and twenty, never fought at about age five. However, of the twenty-nine murderers who were known by the mothers to have fought to some extent, only nine fought once a month or more often. But of the twenty-eight brothers who were known to have fought—the mothers did not know in the cases of three brothers—twenty-two did so once a month or more. In other words, somewhat less than half as many murderers as brothers fought at least once a month. (See Table 15, Appendix A.)

With respect to "talking back" and to certain other aggression outlets considered later in this chapter, the mothers were asked to choose one of four categories of prevalence: frequently, occasionally, almost never, and never. When this was done, the mothers were left to define the categories as they wished. In the case of their sons "talking back" to them, the mothers reported that a lesser number of murderers than of control brothers used this outlet frequently or occasionally. The differences are not significant at the five per cent level. Nevertheless, the mothers judged that only twelve murderers as compared to twenty brothers "talked back" to a frequent or occasional extent. However, only one of the 102 individuals was said by the mothers to have "talked back" frequently. This is indicative of a more general situation in the early lives of the murderers and their brothers: most of the mothers were strict with them and in face-to-face situations the sons usually did what the mothers told them to do and did it quickly and without argument. In connection with this, the mothers were asked the extent to which their sons obeyed them at age five. The mothers said that forty-three murderers and forty-eight brothers obeyed them "almost always" or "usually." Therefore, it would seem that, while both murderers and brothers sometimes did not obey their mothers with respect to specific actions, as a general rule they obeyed them well. In fact, in cases where the sons did things of which the mothers did not approve, the mothers usually had not warned them beforehand. What one murderer said about this point is fairly typical of what a number said:

"Mother was strict with us, all right. But some of the time you didn't know until you'd done something that it was wrong. We'd do what she said, we were afraid not to. But sometimes she didn't say. And then there'd be a scene every time."

My feeling is that most of the mothers were overly strict with both the murderers and the control brothers. Yet, as the murderer quoted above indicated, the mothers tended to be inconsistent in that they frequently did not make their standards of behavior known until after the fact. Both of these approaches, undue strictness and inconsistency, are frustrating to children. The murderers, already greatly frustrated, seem to have resented this strictness and inconsistency more than their brothers. Frustration added on frustration is like opening a wound that is just beginning to heal; resentment results.

However, the mothers had also made the murderers and the brothers especially dependent on them in an emotional sense. They had done this by withholding affection when their sons acted in ways they, the mothers, disapproved. And the mothers gave affection when the sons' behavior was approved by them. Thus, both murderers and brothers usually followed their mothers' wishes, obeyed them. But the murderers, because of their greater over-all frustration, were perhaps more resentful of doing so. Later, this resentment would be added fuel driving them to kill.

When a child of about five is "dressed up" and repeatedly gets his clothes dirty, this can be taken as a form of aggression. In this regard and according to the mothers, the murderers were more extreme, in both directions, than the brothers. Twelve murderers, as compared to four brothers, dirtied their clothes "almost always" or "usually." But only fifteen murderers, as against thirty brothers, did this "about half the time" or "occasionally." Yet, twenty-four murderers and sixteen brothers "almost never" dirtied their clothes. (In the case of the one remaining control brother, the mother said that he was never "dressed up.") These differences are significant at the one per cent level, as Table 16, Appendix A, indicates.

Perhaps the explanation here is that while many of the murders seldom used this channel of release at all, once a murderer did use it to any extent, he persisted in order to aggravate his mother. Certainly getting clothes dirty when "dressed up" contains a component of aggression directed against the mother by the child.

Using the mothers' judgments as the basis, the murderers when about age seventeen generally participated in athletics to a significantly lesser extent than the control brothers. In the cases of six murderers, the mothers did not know whether they had participated in athletics. This was because the murderers were either in prison or otherwise away from home. Making allowance for this, 60 per cent of the murderers, twenty-seven out of forty-five, took part in various athletics "frequently" or "occasionally." But, 78 per cent of the brothers, forty out of fifty-one, used this channel of aggression release "frequently" or "occasionally." At the other end of the scale, 40 per cent of the forty-five murderers "almost never" or "never" participated in athletics; the figure for the fifty-one brothers was 22 per cent. Table 17, Appendix A, shows that these differences are significant at the five per cent level.

Athletics are, in our society, the almost perfect outlet for

146

aggressive feelings. Athletics and the competition they involve are highly approved by the society. The physical energy expended directly or indirectly against opponents can serve quite clearly as an escape valve for aggression. However, the murderers made relatively little use of that escape valve. This cannot be explained on the basis of incapacity due to physical deformity or ill health; there were not enough murderers so incapacitated at age seventeen. It might be partially explained in terms of the fact that most athletics require a degree of social participation ability which the murderers lacked. But I think the major explanation has to do with the fears of the murderers toward becoming violently aggressive once they began to follow some acceptable pattern of aggression release. They tended, by and large, to choose solitary channels of release. Later, I shall consider further this matter of the murderers' fear of becoming violently aggressive.

Hunting is an example of a type of aggression release which from the individual's point of view is, by and large, a solitary one. And, while many hunters would not readily agree, hunting is in great part really a socially acceptable way of venting aggression. At the same time, it does not put the individual in a position where his aggression is likely to get out of hand—except for the remote possibility that he might shoot a human. According to the mothers, the murderers at about age seventeen made considerable use of this form of release, given the fact that many lived in highly urbanized areas which allowed little easy opportunity for hunting.

The mothers said they did not know whether seven of the murderers and two of the brothers had hunted. Of the remaining cases, 36 per cent of the murderers and 18 per cent of the brothers were judged by the mothers to have hunted occasionally or more often. But 64 per cent of the murderers as compared to 82 per cent of the brothers were reported to have hunted almost never or never. (Table 18, Appendix A.)

A number of the murderers with whom I talked expressed an almost fanatical liking for hunting. One man, a quiet middle-aged farmer who shot and killed his wife, said, his eyes lighting up, "Oh, I love hunting. I'd rather do that than anything I can think of. Out there by yourself, in the woods, nothing to worry about."

"How do you feel about animals in general, apart from hunting?" I asked him.

"I like them. Always have. Why, when I was a kid I always had pets around. Always."

"But, in a way, doesn't hunting go against that?"

"No! Why should it? It's different. They're not pets. You don't know them."

Another type of aggression which I would classify as socially acceptable behavior in adolescence is that of mildly antagonizing others by verbal means. This includes what is commonly known as "having a sharp tongue" but does not include the verbal baiting of others to the point where they are exasperated in the extreme. The group of murderers were reported by the mothers to have employed this outlet somewhat less than did their brothers. Although the differences are not statistically significant at the five per cent level, seven out of forty-three murderers, or 16 per cent, used mild verbal antagonism "frequently" or "occasionally," while twelve out of forty-eight brothers, or 25 per cent, did so. (Data were not available in the cases of eight murderers and three brothers.)

Of the nine socially acceptable channels of aggression release, then, the murderers employed four to a significantly lesser degree than their brothers: verbal loudness at age five, releasing anger verbally at age five, physical fighting at age five, and participation in athletics at age seventeen. The murderers used two other channels to a lesser degress than the brothers—"talking back" to the mother at age five and mildly antagonizing others by verbal means at age seventeen—but the differences were not statistically significant. The murderers employed one channel—dirtying clothes when "dressed up" at age five—in such a way that a number of them used it more frequently than the brothers and a number used it less frequently, while the brothers made a "middle-range" use of it. The two remaining channels—anger short of temper tantrums at age five and hunting at age seventeen

—were used to a greater extent by the murderer group than by the control brothers.

An Index of Acceptable Aggression Release was constructed. A given murderer or control brother received one point for each of the previously mentioned nine aggression outlets which he was reported to have employed to a high degree. (See "The Index of Acceptable Aggression Release" in Appendix B for details.) The minimum possible score on this index was zero and the maximum nine. The number of control brothers with relatively high scores was significantly greater than the number of murderers with high scores. Twenty-one brothers had scores of four or more while only eleven brothers had such scores. The mean score for the brothers was 3.5; for the murderers it was 2.5. By and large, the brothers seem to have made more use of acceptable channels of aggression release during their preadult years than did the murderers. (Consult Table 19 in Appendix A for the full distribution of scores.)

Consider now the seven types of aggression release classified as socially unacceptable. The first of these is lying to the mother at age five. The mothers remembered the murderers as having done this much more often, as a group, than had the brothers. Over twice as many murderers as control brothers—sixteen as compared to seven—were said by the mothers to have lied to them "occasionally" or "frequently." Conversely, a substantially greater number of brothers than murderers—forty-four to thirty-five—lied "almost never" or "never." (Using a two-by-two table, $X^2 = 4.548$, $P < 0.05$.)

As I have stated, I think the murderers tended to be basically very aggressive toward their mothers yet feared the latter's disapproval. Lying can be, at the time of commission, a form of aggression which seems to entail no disapproval. After all, the lie may never be found out. It would appear, then, that lying to the mothers was viewed by at least some of the murderers as covert, something which might never be recognized for what it was.

Actually, I discussed this point with only a few murderers.

Perhaps my interpretation is very wide of the mark. However, one of the murderers with whom I discussed the matter, an intelligent, educated man, said, "Yes, I don't like to admit it, but the truth is, when I was a kid I lied to my mother a lot. I had a—almost an urge to do it. Looking back on it, I know she did her best with us. But at the time I thought she was pretty unreasonable, pretty strict, and I—well, I guess I wanted to get back at her."

"How did she react when she found out you'd lied to her?" I asked him.

"She'd get very upset. Tell me I was no son of hers. I remember, that was a favorite saying with her."

"How would you feel when she got upset?"

He was a man who had been in prison eleven years, was middle-aged now, was very correct in most things he did. He put his hands over his eyes for a moment, formulating his answer. "The truth is, I felt bad about it and I felt good about it, too."

Stealing at about the age of five is another form of unacceptable aggression release. To me, stealing, especially by children, is quite distinctly a way of attempting to siphon off antagonistic feelings. It usually involves, also, a striving for approval through the acquisition of material things. But the aggression is, I feel, always there. Here, as with lying, the child can readily assume, at the conscious level, that he will not be discovered. In any event, six of the murderers and only one brother stole "occasionally" or "frequently," the mothers reported. (The remainder "never" or "almost never" stole.) The seven sons stole small amounts of money in the home and small goods —candy, toys, and the like—from neighborhood stores.

Several of the mothers indicated that they had been extremely shocked by this stealing. For example:

"This man, the man who owned the candy store, he came to me and said—he was nice enough about it—'I don't like to tell you this, Mrs. Flannagan,' he said, 'but your boy, Bobby, he's been stealing regular from the store.' I've never gotten over it, not to this day."

"What did you say or do to Bobby?" I asked Mrs. Flannagan.

150

Bobby—Robert Flannagan—had, many years after this incident, when he was thirty, gone into a strange woman's apartment and beaten her to death.

"I lost my temper, I was that upset. I took a stick to him, the only time I ever beat him like that."

"Did you say anything to him?"

"No, I was that upset."

"Did you cry?"

"I came near to it. For two, three days I wasn't myself."

"Because Bobby had been stealing?"

"Yes, that's what I'm saying."

Most mothers would be upset to find their children had been stealing. But I wonder how many would lose their temper, beat the child, become upset for a prolonged period, yet never talk to him about the matter.

A third form of unacceptable aggression release in a child of five is swearing. The mothers said that very few of the murderers or their brothers swore to any extent at that age. Two of the murderers and three of the brothers swore "occasionally." None of either group swore "frequently," according to the mothers. The mothers as a group tended to register horror at the idea of children swearing. As has been pointed out, neither the murderers nor their brothers seemed, generally, to be the type of children who wanted directly to incur their mothers' disapproval. Perhaps they seldom swore when near the mothers for that reason.

Temper tantrums, a fourth unacceptable form of behavior, were reported to have been manifested by a strikingly greater number of the murderers than of the control brothers. Seventeen murderers as compared to two brothers had temper tantrums once or more during childhood. (Using a two-by-two table—presence of tantrums and absence of tantrums versus the number of murderers and the number of control brothers—the differences are significant at the one per cent level. $X^2 = 14.552$.)

Temper tantrums are obviously a way of releasing aggression. I think the high prevalence among the murderers is accounted for by the fact that they had more aggression bottled up within them as children than did the brothers, yet were afraid to release it. Therefore, it burst its bounds in an uncontrollable, violent behavior pattern as tantrums.

Twelve of the seventeen murderers who had tantrums had them once a week or more often during the period when the tantrums were at their height. Neither of the two control brothers who had tantrums had them that often.

Only a small minority of children who have severe tantrums later commit murder, of course. The same is true for convulsive seizures, discussed in a previous chapter. However, the sudden, violent, out-of-control qualities of both tantrums and convulsions are evident in most actual acts of murder.

While interviewing murderers and reading biographies of them I was especially struck by one fact: their highly ambivalent approach to animals. They seemed to have an unusually strong liking for animals. Yet, often they had hurt them. Apart from hurting them in the usual sense, quite a number of the murderers had been abnormally preoccupied with hunting, as noted previously.

Thus, a fifth form of unacceptable aggression release investigated was the matter of deliberately hurting animals in other than hunting situations. I knew that the mothers would in all likelihood not know of all the instances where the murderers and brothers had, as children and adolescents, hurt animals. Nevertheless, it was important to find out what incidents of this nature they did know about. The mothers said that five of the murderers had deliberately and seriously hurt animals once or more. They did not know of any instances where the control brothers had done this. Perhaps the brothers were more secretive, but I doubt it. At the same time, the mothers reported that in general the murderers treated animals better in childhood than did the brothers (see table on page 153).

The murderers, then, appear to have been much more extreme in their reactions to animals. A significantly greater number of them than of the brothers treated animals "extremely well," as the table shows. Yet five murderers were known to have hurt animals. And those five were among the forty-one who generally treated them "extremely well."

There comes to mind the case of a sixteen-year-old boy who raped, and then slowly cut to death over a two-day period, a twenty-year-old girl. During the two days and for some time after, the boy carried pieces of the girl around in his pockets. (The boy was found to be legally sane; he was sentenced to life imprisonment.)

	Number of Murderers	Number of Brothers
Extremely Well	41	27
Moderately Well *	5	23
Badly *	0	0
Unknown **	5	1
Total	51	51
$X^2 = 14.324$	P $<$ 0.01	

* Combined for X^2 calculation.
** Not included in X^2 calculation.

As a child, this boy seemed, most of the time, to love animals. He had several dogs, several cats, a pet snake. He brought home a crow with a badly broken wing and nursed it back to health. Yet he had cut cats to pieces.

I suspect the explanation for this type of behavior lies in the following: excessive aggression leads to fantasies of torturing animals and humans. The fantasies lead to guilt feelings. The guilt feelings are partially expiated by kindness to animals. But occasionally the aggression overrides all else, and the fantasies are made real by actual, overt behavior.

Fist fighting at about age seventeen, a sixth form of socially unacceptable behavior, was apparently employed as an aggression vent with approximately equal infrequency by the murderers and the control brothers. Thirty-four murderers and thirty-two brothers were reported as never having fought during that period. Five of the murderers and six of the brothers got in an occasional fight but none fought with any such frequency as once every few days. In the cases of the remaining twelve murderers and thirteen brothers, the mothers said they simply did not know.

Of course, this is a behavioral area where the mothers would be somewhat unlikely to have the full facts. Perhaps some of the thirty-four murderers and thirty-two brothers whom the mothers believed never to have fought actually did so without the mothers having any knowledge of it. On the other hand, most of the families lived in neighborhoods where the parents would learn quickly of fights in which their sons had been engaged.

Given extreme frustration in early life, aggressiveness is likely to manifest itself when later the individual becomes intoxicated. Therefore the mothers were questioned concerning the extent to which their sons became intoxicated and whether they then became aggressive. The questions were limited to the period when the sons were less than twenty years old because it was not likely the mothers would have information relative to older ages; frequently, the sons would have left home by then. Intoxication was defined for the mothers as existent when the sons' verbal or other behavior became noticeably different from the usual due to the intake of alcohol. As to the matter of aggressiveness, I am speaking here of extreme verbal antagonism and of physical assault other than fist fighting, the latter having been dealt with already.

The mothers said that seventeen of the murderers and nine of the control brothers were known by them to have become intoxicated once or more during adolescence, before the age of twenty. A majority of the seventeen murderers and of the nine brothers became intoxicated more than once, but not as frequently as once a week. It is reasonable to suppose that more of the murderers than of the brothers became intoxicated in adolescence because of their greater need for the reduction of anxiety, that anxiety being bound up with aggressive feelings as a result of extreme frustration. But how many of the murderers and brothers became violently aggressive when intoxicated? According to the mothers' answers to questioning, ten of the seventeen murderers and two of the nine brothers did so; the remaining seven murderers and seven brothers did not. (Using a two-by-two table, $X^2 = 3.161$, $P > 0.05$.)

Thus, the murderers used five of the unacceptable aggression outlets in definitely greater numbers than did the brothers. These outlets were: lying, stealing, temper tantrums, hurting animals, and violent aggression when intoxicated. On the other hand, very few of the murderers and almost equally few of the brothers employed the two remaining channels: swearing, and fist fighting at age seventeen.

An Index of Unacceptable Aggression Release was constructed in the same manner as was the Index of Acceptable Aggression Release. The individual, murderer or brother, received one point for each of the seven unacceptable aggression outlets which he was reported to have used to a high degree. (See "The Index of Unacceptable Aggression Release" in Appendix B for details.) The maximum score an individual could receive was seven while the minimum was zero.

With respect to this index, there were a significantly greater number of murderers than of brothers with high scores. Seventeen murderers out of fifty-one had scores of two or more. Only four brothers out of fifty-one had scores at that level. Also, the mean score for the murderer group was three times higher than for the control brother group: 1.2 and 0.4 respectively. (Consult Table 20 in Appendix A for the total distribution of scores and for the chi-square figure.) According to the mothers, the murderers quite definitely employed the seven unacceptable aggression outlets during childhood and adolescence to a greater degree than did the brothers.

The scores of individual murderers and brothers on the two aggression release indices were combined to provide an Index of General Aggression Release. Here the maximum possible score was sixteen while the minimum was zero. The chi-square figure in Table 21, Appendix A, is significant at the five per cent level. However, in this instance that proves little because there is no consistent trend in the distribution. For given index scores there are more murderers or more brothers, but neither murderers nor brothers tend to have high or low scores. Twenty-six murderers as compared to twenty-five brothers had scores of four or more. And the mean score for the murderer group was 3.6 while for the control brother group it was 4.0. The use by the murderers of the unacceptable aggression releases tended approximately to balance out the use by the control brothers of the acceptable aggression releases. With respect to general release, as measured in this index, the control group experienced more than the murderer group, but only slightly so. By and large, the murderers used one type of release and the brothers used the other, but the total release was about the same.

Why was it that the murderers tended to be overconformists a great deal of the time, avoiding even socially acceptable aggression releases, and yet used relatively extreme and unacceptable releases the rest of the time? I think they were frequently conformists and avoided the acceptable outlets because they had both strong drives to aggress and fears that once they began they could not call a halt. At the same time, their tremendous reservoir of aggression had to have some escape. So, occasionally, it would burst forth, in tantrums or other unacceptable ways, regardless of the murderers' fears.

Once the aggression did burst forth, there was the reward of temporarily getting rid of anxiety. And there was the further reward of, in effect, aggressing against the society that had frustrated them. Of course, there would be retaliation from the society, from agents of the society. And, in a way, that too was reward; the murderers felt some guilt at having expressed their aggression violently, and the guilt would be partially expiated. Yet, in the future they would in general continue to avoid acceptable channels. Perhaps this was because of the unconscious fear that they would not be able to stop with acceptable or minor unacceptable releases but would go on to the most unacceptable of all: murder.

In Chapter 1 it was stated that aggression release was treated in this study as a control variable with respect to the central hypothesis: that the preadult frustration of murderers is significantly greater than that of nonmurderers. It was necessary, then, to hold aggression release during childhood and adolescence approximately constant by statistical means while investigating the degree of association between general frustration and presence or absence of murder.

This was done by dividing the total group of 102 subjects, murderers and control brothers, into two subgroups. One subgroup of murderers and brothers was composed of individuals who made use of socially acceptable and unacceptable aggression releases extensively. Extensively was defined as a score of four or more on the Index of General Aggression Release. The other subgroup was made up of individuals who employed aggression releases infrequently. Infrequently was defined in terms of a score of three or less on the Index of General Aggression Release.

There were fifty-one individuals in each of the two subgroups. The figure fifty-one was the same as the numbers of murderers and control brothers due to coincidence only. Two chi-square tests were made: one for the "extensive aggression release" subgroup and one for the "infrequent aggression release" subgroup. Thus it could be determined in each of the two instances whether the relationship between general frustration and presence or absence of murder was significant.

Among the fifty-one murderers and control brothers who used socially acceptable and unacceptable aggression outlets extensively in childhood and adolescence, the group of twenty-six murderers had significantly higher scores on the Index of General Frustration than did the brothers. (Chi-square significant at the one per cent level. See Table 22, Appendix A.) Further, among the fifty-one murderers and control brothers who used socially acceptable and unacceptable aggression outlets infrequently, the group of twenty-five murderers had somewhat higher scores on the Index of General Frustration than did the brothers. (Chi-square not significant at the five per cent level. See Table 23, Appendix A.) Put another way, when aggression releases were used extensively, the central hypothesis of the study is confirmed. However, when aggression releases were used infrequently, the central hypothesis is not confirmed.

The Case of Harold Wesson

HAROLD WESSON is not one of the fifty-one murderers in the sample used in this study. He is over seventy years of age; his mother died many years ago. However, his case is an illuminating one in many respects, including those related to aggression release.

Harold Wesson was born in 1886, brought up on a small farm in Maine. The farm was a poor one, and to make ends meet Harold's father operated a small grocery store in the near-by town. The father spent long hours at the store; as Harold grew up he saw little of his father. What he does remember of his father is that he was a quiet man, never seemed to get upset about anything.

Harold's mother ruled the household. She was not loud, she did not rant and rave, but in a quiet forceful way she dominated everyone around her.

Harold was the baby of the family; there were two older sisters. His earliest memories, at age four, are of his mother telling him not to do this or that, that he would get hurt. She would not let him play with other children, kept him close to her. She had been a schoolteacher, and when he was four she began teaching him to read and write, add and subtract. By the time he was seven he could do these things quite well. She kept him out of school the first year, saying that there was no need for him to go, he knew everything they would teach him in the first grade. So, at seven, he started school in the second grade.

Now, in his seventies, Harold Wesson remembers vividly that first day in school. As he sat through the morning's classes, he began to sense that the other students, and the teacher as well, resented his starting in the second grade. At eleven-thirty the school bell rang. Harold picked up his lunch box and started out of the classroom, heading for home. He thought school was over for the day; his mother had not explained to him that he was to eat the contents of the lunch box at school.

The teacher came running after him, caught up with him, and brought him back to the classroom.

"Where were you going, Harold?" she asked him, in front of the other children.

"Home."

"But we don't go home until three o'clock."

"I thought school was over."

The other children began to laugh. He heard one say, "He's not smart enough to start in the second grade."

"No, Harold," the teacher said. "School is not over. We eat our lunch here. Now eat your lunch and then we'll have more lessons. And I think you're going to need them if you're to start in the second grade."

Harold was thoroughly humiliated. Looking back on the incident, after more than sixty years, he says, "I felt as small as an ant. I could have crawled into the floor. It took me several years to get over it."

As he went through the early grammar school grades, Harold's mother made him come home directly after school every day. She seldom set him to doing any chores; she just wanted him with her. She was an intensely moral woman and she spent long periods telling him what were the right and wrong ways to act in life.

There in the prison, when I was interviewing Harold Wesson, I asked him, "How did your mother act when you didn't do what she wanted you to do? Did she punish you?"

An old man wearing a hearing aid, fat, but with quick piercing eyes, he looked up abruptly and then back, as it were, over sixty years. "That was the trouble," he said. "She never punished me. No reason to. I always did what she said. I wouldn't have dared to do anything else."

He sat in thought for a moment, breathing slowly, heavily. Then he said, "I never did anything wrong in my whole life. Never. Except that one time when I—when I did what got me in here." He shook his head and laughed slightly. "I've never done

anything wrong except that one time. I've never broken a regulation here in the prison in forty years. Check my record. You'll
see."

In his prison file there is only one recorded instance of his
having violated even the most minor regulation.

When Harold was nine his mother was told by the family
doctor that she had cancer. For the next eight years she was in
bed continuously. She had nine operations. When Harold was
seventeen she died. But during those years when she was bed-
ridden, she insisted that Harold be with her almost constantly
except for the hours when he was in school or sleeping. She never
asked him to do very much. She just wanted him near her. She
was always afraid he'd get hurt if he were out somewhere. When
he was in high school she wouldn't let him play on any of the
athletic teams. He never had a date. His mother told him young
men did not go out with girls until they were engaged. He never
thought to do other than what she told him. His main interest
during those years was reading. He read widely; he read most of
Shakespeare; he read Dickens, Tolstoy, Poe.

And then, in June of 1904, in the same month that he graduated from high school, Harold's mother died. He felt very badly
but, also, he felt free for the first time in his life. He had done
well in school and, although he had little money, he decided
to attend a near-by state university. That summer his father died.

Harold entered the university in the fall of 1904. He found
a job stoking a furnace nightly in one of the large buildings on
the campus. Actually, the work was not hard, and, since he slept
in the building, he had enough money to get by. During his
first two years of college, he studied very little. He felt free and
and he spent most of his days simply idling. He read what appealed to him; he went for long walks. After his freshman year
he joined a fraternity. He took an interest in athletics, began to
play on the fraternity tennis and basketball teams.

His grades during his freshman year were adequate. But in
his sophomore year his lack of study began to take effect and his
grades slipped badly. He realized that if he were to be allowed
to stay in college he would have to apply himself. And beginning
in his junior year he did so. From that point on his grades were

extraordinarily high. Harold Wesson was, and is, an extremely intelligent man. His over-all I.Q., as measured by the prison psychologists, is 142, higher than more than 99 per cent of the United States population.

Harold was majoring in English and he took a course in Elizabethan drama with a professor whom he grew to respect highly. Harold had been developing a growing interest in the theater and it suddenly came to him, one day in the spring of his junior year, that he would make the theater his life's work. He would be a playwright. He asked the English professor if during the next year he could write a play as his senior thesis. The professor said yes, he thought that was a fine idea.

During that summer Harold began to outline his play, write trial scenes. But when he returned to the university in the fall, the professor was not there. He had taken a position at another university. There was no other faculty member qualified to direct Harold's thesis.

Harold immediately gave up the idea of writing a play and never, during the ensuing years, did he do anything active toward reaching his goal of becoming a playwright.

When I was interviewing him I asked, "Why was it that you didn't go ahead and write a play? There might have been some-one else around the university who could have helped you."

He waved one hand and chuckled. "That's the way I've always been. I get enthused about something and then the least thing comes along to throw it off and I'm down in the dumps. Way down. And I never do anything about it again. That's the way I am."

"Did you make any friendships with female students when you were in college?" I asked him.

"No. No. There weren't many of them there. Ten or fifteen, that's all. It wasn't like it is now. But then, too, it was my mother's influence, I suppose, even though she had died. As I said, she'd always told me never to go out with girls until I was engaged to one." He laughed and looked up with his piercing eyes. "Of course, it's kind of hard to get engaged without first going out with a girl. But my mother didn't look at it that way. Little gaps in logic like that never bothered her. But that was the trouble, you see. I always tried to do just what she told me. Except that one time. When I lost control of myself."

After graduating from college, Harold had no clear idea of what profession he wanted to follow. He took a job in a brokerage house. He did not particularly like the work but nothing else appealed to him more. Though he never attempted any playwriting, he maintained his interest in the theater. He read plays, studied them, and occasionally on weekends he went to New York to the theater.

After he had been in the brokerage house nearly three years, it occurred to Harold that teaching was something which might interest him. He applied to a teachers' agency and soon found a position as an English teacher at the Greymount School for girls.

At that time Harold Wesson was an exceedingly handsome young man. He was small, about five-feet six, weighed one hundred and twenty pounds. But he had deep brown eyes, regular features, and a most ingratiating smile. He was the type of young man who appears to be a highly sensitive person, yet not effeminate. Dr. James Taggart, headmaster at Greymount, was pleased to have him on the staff.

Practically all of the teaching staff were women. Harold soon became good friends with several of them. One was a Miss Ruth Johnson, about forty, the assistant headmistress of Greymount. A second was Miss Francis, a history teacher in her late twenties. A third was Miss Myers. Julia Myers, like Harold, was new at Greymount. This gave them a common bond and they became particularly good friends.

During Harold Wesson's first year at Greymount, this little group of four—Miss Johnson, Miss Francis, Julia Myers, and Harold—were often together. They went to meals together; they went to dances and to various community activities together. And usually, within the four, Julia Myers and Harold were more or less paired off.

Twenty-eight years later, in prison, Harold Wesson wrote a brief autobiography. In it, he explained his relationship to Julia Myers. The following is a paraphrase of what he wrote:

162

"Miss Myers and I were good friends from the beginning. There was never any sort of romantic attachment between us at all and in fact I might say that we were simply good friends. Just to prove the point, I never even put my arm around her. And I never once called her Julia. Always Miss Myers. Sometimes I thought she might have had some romantic inclination toward me although I could never be sure about that but I certainly know that I never did about her. Sometimes she used to suggest things that made me wonder a little but I acted as if I didn't notice. For example, one evening we had been to a church supper and I think she said as we started home something such as: Why don't we walk back through the woods, it's so nice there now, and the others will never miss us? I said immediately: No, I think we'd better not. People might begin to talk, Miss Myers."

During the spring of his second year at Greymount, Harold received a letter from Julia Myers which surprised him greatly. In it she said: "Please stop forcing yourself on me. I want to feel free to go with whomever I like. So please leave me alone."

Harold was extremely hurt that Julia Myers would feel he had been forcing himself on her. The next day he caught up with her as she was returning to her room from breakfast.

"Miss Myers, that was an awfully mean thing to do, to write me that letter."

Now, over forty years later, Harold Wesson says he remembers Julia Myers' reaction as clearly as if it were yesterday. She looked around to be sure no one was in sight and then she put the tips of her fingers on his left forearm and said, "I'm sorry, Harold. I couldn't help it. Miss Johnson made me write that letter. She said there had to be a stop put to our seeing each other so much."

"Then we're still good friends? You're not angry at me?"

"No, of course not. Only we mustn't see so much of each other for a while."

Harold felt much better then. That afternoon he went to the office of Miss Johnson, the assistant headmistress, and knocked on the door.

Harold went directly up to her and said, "Miss Johnson, I think that was a terrible thing to do, make Miss Myers write that letter."

"What letter?"

"Saying that I should stop forcing myself on Miss Myers."

"I did no such thing!" Miss Johnson stood up, her face red. "Though you have been seeing entirely too much of her. And if you ask me, I think you have been forcing yourself on her. In fact, you've been forcing yourself on all of us."

"I'm sorry. I didn't realize I had been," Harold said, shocked. Miss Johnson did not answer. "But you didn't make Miss Myers write that letter to me?" Harold asked.

"Of course not. I knew nothing about it."

Harold left Miss Johnson's office. He did not know what to think. He was very upset. He remembers that he felt strongly like committing suicide. But he did nothing except to avoid Julia Myers and Miss Johnson for several weeks.

About a month later there was a community dance. Harold went by himself. Julia Myers and Miss Johnson were there. He looked over at them and they smiled at him. He asked Julia Myers if he might dance with her and she said yes. It was the first time they had talked together since that morning when he had asked her about the letter. Now, she seemed quite friendly. At the end of the dance there was an intermission. Harold remembers that he asked Julia if he might have the next dance and she said she would like that. He then returned her to where she had been sitting with Ruth Johnson.

When the next dance began, Harold looked for Julia but could not find her. Finally he saw her. She and Ruth Johnson were dancing together. Harold could not understand it. When the dance ended, he went up to them and said to Julia, "Miss Myers, you agreed that this dance was to be with me."

Julia Myers glanced quickly at Ruth Johnson and answered, "I did not say that!"

"But——"

"I thought we made it clear to you once before," Ruth Johnson interrupted, "that we do not like you forcing yourself on us."

Harold turned, walked away, and left the dance. About this incident, Harold later wrote much as follows in his autobiography: "Now what the dickens was I to think? I didn't know what to believe and I was extremely upset. That night I decided that the only thing for me to do was to go and see Miss Myers' mother, who lived in New York, and since the next day was a Friday I made plans for the weekend. I thought that I wouldn't discuss with Miss Myers the fact that I was going to see her mother but I would leave a note explaining about it. I wanted to leave her a present with the note so I went into town and bought her a kind of thermos jug in a leather case which I was able to get her initials stamped on in gold while I waited.

"I left the thermos jug and the note in her room and took the train to New York and when I arrived I telephoned Mrs. Myers and she agreed to see me. Mrs. Myers was a very sophisticated woman, dowagerish I should say, looking back on it.

"We had a most pleasant conversation (we had tea), and I explained to her that my intentions toward her daughter were entirely honorable, that I had never even called her Julia, and that I had never meant to force myself on her. Mrs. Myers said that she understood and that it was perfectly all right with her for me to go on seeing her daughter as long as I did not continue to give her expensive presents. (I didn't tell her about the thermos jug.)"

When Harold returned to the Greymount School he found the jug in its initialed leather case in his room, returned by Julia Myers.

The next morning he asked Miss Johnson if she knew why Julia Myers had returned the jug.

"I certainly do," said Ruth Johnson. "Miss Myers is angry with you and for good reason."

"Why?"

"Why? Because you went to see her mother without even talking it over with her first."

"I left her a note." Miss Johnson did not answer. "Do you think she'll speak to me?" Harold asked.

"No, I don't," Miss Johnson said and walked on.

During the next weeks, Harold stayed by himself much of

the time and brooded about the disintegration of his friendship with Julia Myers and Ruth Johnson. Occasionally he saw Miss Francis, the young history teacher who had been the third girl of the little group with whom Harold had originally been friends.

After several weeks had passed Harold asked Miss Francis if she would try to help him regain the friendship of Julia Myers and Miss Johnson. She said she would try. Harold suggested that they all have a picnic at a camp beside a near-by lake owned by the school. Miss Francis agreed to invite Julia Myers and Miss Johnson. They said they would come.

This was in the early summer of the year 1914. Harold planned the picnic carefully. The girls were to meet him at the lake at four-thirty in the afternoon. He would bring the necessary food. They would all fish and cook the catch for dinner.

Harold was there at four o'clock, getting everything in readiness. Four-thirty came but the girls did not appear. Harold waited and grew restless. He was afraid they would not come. Five-thirty came and still there was no sign of them. Finally at six o'clock they arrived. Harold was very upset but he tried not to show it. The girls seemed unconscious of the fact that they had arrived so late. Harold mentioned something to the effect that it was getting pretty late to fish. The girls agreed. Harold said he had brought some canned meat along and they could have that for dinner.

Then Harold asked the girls if they would like to play some games before dinner. They said they would. Harold had been in charge of entertainment in his college fraternity and apparently he had in mind some of the milder games used at initiations. One of these was to see who could most quickly push a penny the length of a table top with his nose. Another involved a person putting some cotton in his mouth, then blowing it up into the air for a second person to catch in his mouth.

Harold Wesson explained the games to the girls and said that Miss Francis and Julia Myers should play the game where one pushed the penny with the nose. He asked them to go outside for a few minutes while he and Miss Johnson prepared for the other game. They thought this an odd request but did as he asked.

Harold took a wad of cotton from the carrying pack he had brought and began to place it in Ruth Johnson's mouth. She bit down hard on his right forefinger and yelled, "What kind of funny business do you think you're——"

Harold hit her on the side of the face with his right fist. He went berserk. He grabbed her throat with his left hand, forced the cotton into her mouth, choking her. He picked up a stick leaning against the wall of the cabin and hit her over the head with great force five or six times.

Julia Myers and Miss Francis ran in. Harold hit Miss Francis with the stick several times, knocked her unconscious. Then he hit Julia Myers with his fist, dragged her into the bedroom, threw her on the bed, and bound her hands and feet to the bedposts. He ran out, bound Miss Francis' hands. He ran to the kitchen, picked up a carving knife, went back to the bedroom, and wildly cut the clothing from Julia Myers. Then he threw himself on her and raped her.

Finally he went outside and sat down on a rock beside the lake. It was very still. There were no sounds except the occasional notes of a bird in the woods.

After some time, Harold, in a trance as if he were a sleep-walker, got in a canoe, paddled mechanically down the lake to the town. He went into a drugstore and telephoned Dr. Taggart, headmaster of the Greymount School.

"Dr. Taggart. This is Harold Wesson. I wish you'd go up to the camp immediately. Something terrible has happened."

"What? What has happened?"

Harold hung up and walked out of the drugstore. He went over to the police station. Police Chief Giles was at his desk.

"What can I do for you, Harold? What's the matter? You don't look so good."

"You'd better lock me up, Mr. Giles," Harold said. "I think I've done something wrong."

Harold was examined by several doctors and found to be legally sane. Supposedly, the prosecuting attorney visited Harold in his cell and said he would make a deal with him. If Harold would plead guilty, it would save the state considerable expense and save the prosecutor's office much time. The prosecutor would see to it that Harold got life imprisonment rather than the death penalty. But Harold would have to promise never to request a pardon. If he did not agree to this, he would certainly get the death sentence; there was the testimony of Julia Myers and Miss Francis.

Harold, in a state of severe depression, is supposed to have agreed. He pleaded guilty and waived trial by jury. He was sentenced to life imprisonment without possibility of parole.

Some forty years later, Harold Wesson told me his version of the crime. We sat in what amounted to his "apartment" in the prison. He had more seniority than any other inmate; he was in effect head of the prison school; he had never caused any trouble; and so he was allowed special privileges. He had four rooms in the old cell block which was otherwise unused now. We sat in a room the size of a large living room. This was his office. There was a desk with a typewriter and "In" and "Out" baskets. There was a workbench with various carpenter's tools on it. There were bookcases, one containing copies of the *National Geographic Magazine* dating back to 1920. Separated from this main room by unlocked but barred doors were three small rooms: Harold's bedroom, a room with a hot plate and cooking supplies, and a storage room.

I sat in the swivel chair by the desk. Harold Wesson sat on a high stool at one corner of the desk.

I offered him a cigarette and he said, "No. Don't smoke."

I lighted my cigarette and he went over to his workbench and got me an ash tray. He wore a white shirt and trousers, unlike the blue denim of most of the other inmates. His stomach strained against his shirt front and hung over his belt. He looked like an old man who has gone to seed except for his eyes which glanced about sharply, never missing anything.

He sat down on the stool again, winced and made a movement toward his back with his left hand. "Back's giving me trouble. Don't know what it is. I've been over to the hospital but they don't know what it is. Or at least they say they don't." He laughed. "Doctors don't know half of what they claim to."

He stopped, and I waited for him to get back to his version of the crime.

"Oh," he said suddenly. "Oh, about what happened. Well, I don't believe half of those things that came out in the papers at the time of the trial. Not half of it. I hit her, I know that. Ruth Johnson, I mean. But I never choked her, and I never hit her with a stick. And I never raped Julia Myers. I'll tell you about that. But about my killing Ruth Johnson. When she bit my finger like that and implied that I was trying some funny business with her, I saw red. I just went out of my head. And I remember taking my fist and hitting her and going on hitting her and then she fell down and I realized what I'd done and I picked her up and propped her against the wall. She wasn't dead then but I killed her—she must have hit her head when I knocked her down —and I admitted it."

"And then what happened?" I asked him.

"What?" The ear his hearing aid was on was turned away from me.

"What happened then?"

"Well, I've never been able to remember clearly. My memory blacked out on me partly. Like being in a room and switching the light on and off. That's what it's like. I remember some things and not others."

"What's the next thing you remember?"

"Well, the other two girls came in. I told them I'd hit Ruth Johnson. But none of us thought she was dead. Then Julia Myers asked me to come into the bedroom with her for a minute. And they said I raped her. Nonsense, I say. You know what happened? She asked me if I wanted her to undress and she said I could do anything I liked with her. Well, I was extremely upset emotionally after having hit Ruth Johnson and after all I was human and I guess I helped her undress. You can believe this or not but I'd never had intercourse with a woman before. I'd never even thought about it because my mother had always made such a point of the fact that people didn't even kiss outside of marriage. And I'd never seen a woman naked before.

"So I helped her undress and I remember I tried to take her shoes off for her and she said, 'Silly, untie the laces first.' We had intercourse once and that was all. I went outside and I felt terrible, worse than I ever had in my life. I sat down on the bank by the stream and then after a while I got in the canoe and I paddled down the lake to the town. That was the hardest thing I ever did in my life."

Harold Wesson looked straight at me. "And if you think it's easy telling you this, you're crazy." He paused. "Anyway, I went into town and I told them I thought they'd better lock me up. Giles, he was the police chief, he didn't want to do it. 'I can't just lock you up, Harold,' he said. 'What have you done?' My memory was blacked out then, you see, and I said, 'I don't know but I have a feeling I've done something terrible.' Finally I talked him into putting me into a cell."

"After you regained your memory," I said, "which made you feel worse, having killed Miss Johnson or having had intercourse with Miss Myers?"

"The intercourse," Harold Wesson answered immediately.

"Why was that?"

"Why? Well, when I hit Ruth Johnson, I'd lost control of myself. I didn't know what I was doing. Of course I shouldn't have done it but I couldn't control myself. With the intercourse, that was different. I was upset but I knew what I was doing and I went ahead anyway."

"Do you think it's ever right for people to have sexual relationships outside of marriage?"

"No, I do not," he answered. "My mother always taught me that. She was too strict about a lot of things but about that she was right."

"What's your opinion about this recent case where that shoe salesman raped the fifteen-year-old girl?"

"He should have been hung. Hung, not given fifteen years. I tell you, this country has gone sex mad. You can't pick up a magazine, you can't pick up a book but what it isn't sex, sex, sex." He groped through the papers and magazines on his desk in order to find something to illustrate his point but then he let the matter go.

"I've been here forty-two years," he said, "and do you think they'd give me a pardon? No. I never made any deal with the prosecutor about not asking for a pardon. That was all a lie. But there are a lot of them have been in here for murder.

Some for two murders, some for murder and sex crimes, some who've been in prison three times before. And they've gotten pardons after eighteen, twenty years."

Harold Wesson slid off the high stool and came toward me. "Listen," he said, "did you know about the case two years ago when Boyce, Gerald Boyce, was pardoned from here? He'd been in prison twice before for armed robbery. Twice. And then he got sent up here for first-degree murder. Well, he'd been here seventeen years when he went up for pardon. I'd been here more than twice that long. Well, anyway, the warden came in here one evening. You know how he walks——" Harold Wesson lumbered around the room in imitation of the warden's gait.

"You haven't lost your sense of humor," I said.

"What?" Wesson looked up quickly. "No, but that's the only thing I've got left. Being in here forty-two years, it takes everything out of you. It takes all your courage away."

He sat down on the stool again and then went on. "The warden came in and he said to me, 'Harold, Boyce just got his pardon.'

"'That so?' I said. 'Shouldn't have. He's a criminal through and through.'

"'Good prison record,' the warden said to me, swaying back and forth on his feet the way he does. Well, I proceeded to tell him a thing or two. I told him Boyce had a good record as far as he knew but there were a lot of things went on in here that he knew nothing about."

"You've been in charge of the education program here for a good many years, haven't you?" I said. There is an education officer at the prison, but Harold Wesson is in direct charge of the program.

"That's right. Forty-one years. I've built it up from nothing. When I came here they taught them how to read and write their name and that was about all."

"I know. I've heard that for a small prison the program is one of the best in the country and that it's largely due to your work."

He looked pleased and said nothing for a moment. Then: "In forty-one years, I've missed one half day. And that was due to some stomach sickness I had." He glanced over at a clock on the wall. "I've got to be over there at three. Open up the library at three-thirty and I always get there a half-hour early and get things ready.

"You see," he said, "when I came here there was nothing in the way of education but a packing crate of books. After I'd been here a year I asked the warden—old Warden Snow it was then —if he'd let me be the teacher. He did and I went to work. I built desks and bookcases and I built tables and chairs. I spent some of my own money and I finally managed to get two hundred dollars a year from the prison budget. I sent for books to these discount houses and I saw that I got my money's worth. I put in a good filing system. And I set up a whole array of good courses. Got good people to teach them too. Grammar school courses on up. Why, I've even got some college courses going here. But does that get me a pardon? No."

"Do you read much?" I asked him.

"Read all the new books that come in. Read *Popular Science* and the *National Geographic*."

"Have you ever done any correspondence courses here in prison yourself?"

"No, nothing much. Oh, I tried it but it didn't work out. After I came here, I wanted to get my M.A. in English literature. I wrote to three universities. They all turned me down. One of them laughed at me. A man in prison trying to get an M.A. That did it. That ended it for me. I lost all hope of ever doing it. Of course, you don't need an M.A. for the kind of teaching you do here. But anyway, that's the way I am. I told you. I get an idea about something and I'm all enthused about it. But then if somebody throws cold water on it, I'm down in the dumps and that's the end of it."

He sat there on the stool thinking, blinking his eyes against the bright light reflected from the snow outside. "Oh, I took a couple of these correspondence courses on how to do things." He chuckled. "You see, they had it set up so you paid so much a month for each course, four dollars I think it was. You could go at your own speed but it was supposed to take about a year. I took a course in radio. I finished it in a month."

"I built a radio receiver here," Wesson went on. "I hooked it up with speakers in every cell so that they could all listen to it. And I took an electrician's course. Finished that in a month too." He shrugged his shoulders. "But I never did much more than that. As I say, you lose all your courage in here. It takes all you've got to keep going, do your work, keep from going neurotic."

He glanced over at the clock again. "I've got to get down to the school pretty quick."

"If you have time, tell me about this girl—Margaret, is it? —who used to come to see you?"

"Margaret?" He settled back on the stool. "What did they tell you about her?" He inclined his head in the general direction of the administration offices of the prison. "Told you I wanted to marry her, didn't they? Ah, they're crazy. I never wanted to marry her. Just want to take care of her. Why, I'm twenty-five years older than she is. What would I want to marry a girl twenty-five years younger than I am for? I'm not that far out of touch with things."

"Look." He nodded toward the barred window. Outside, beyond the high wall and across the snow-covered lawn, was the main highway. Going down it was a big truck, overloaded with Christmas trees. "Going to market," he said. "I've got to see about getting one for here." He reached over to the desk, took a pencil, and made a note on a small pad.

Then he said, "No, you see, Margaret started coming to see me when she was just a little girl, three, four years old. She used to come with her father."

"Who was he?"

"Philip Howard. One of the biggest men in the state before he died three years ago. Well, as I was saying, Phil used to come to see me as regular as clockwork. We'd been classmates down at the university and he never let me down. He'd bring Margaret with him. She was just a little tot at first and pretty as a picture."

He glanced over at the clock. It was five past three now, but he went on, wanting to talk about Margaret. "Week after week they'd come, her getting bigger all the time. I could almost see her growing. Well, then in 1935, I think it was, Phil took sick. Cerebral hemorrhage. Half paralyzed. Margaret was about twenty then. She kept on coming to see me. Every week. Now, there was never anything between us like they'll tell you out there. We were friends, good friends, and that was all.

"After the war started she met this young fellow. William Hestler was his name. He was a lieutenant in the Army. I never met him but, anyway, Margaret married him. I was glad she did. I wanted to see her get married and have children. Well, he went overseas to the Pacific. She had a little baby. But after she was out of the hospital she kept right on coming to see me. Every Saturday.

"Then she heard on the radio this commentator, what's his name? I don't remember. Well, it doesn't matter. Anyway she heard her husband's Army outfit was trapped on some island and about to be wiped out. When she heard that, she went out of her head, had a nervous breakdown. They put her in a nursing home. I wanted to get out of here, get a pardon and take care of her, but they wouldn't let me. Then when the war was over, her husband did come back. He was all right after all. They had another baby but they couldn't get along. Wasn't his fault as far as I know. I think it was because she never fully got over that breakdown. Anyway, in 1947 they got a divorce.

"After that she used to come to see me regularly again. Bring the children sometimes too. Why, one year we had a Christmas party. Right here, right in this room. Margaret came with her mother, sister, and the two children. The six of us had a party right in this room. I decorated the place and I had a Christmas tree over in that corner. The warden let us have Christmas dinner served right in here. We played games afterwards and sang carols."

He looked out of the window. "It was the nicest time I ever had," he said. "The nicest time anywhere, in or out of prison."

He was lost in memory and then he stirred himself, glanced over at the clock, and slid off the stool. "I've got to go. Got to open up the library."

"What happened to Margaret?" I asked. "She's in the mental hospital, isn't she?"

"Yes, they put her in there but they shouldn't have. That's why I want to get out, get a pardon, to get her out of there."

He sat down on a corner of the desk. "You see, in 1950 they claimed she got worse. Her family claimed they couldn't manage her and they put her in there. Well, she did need treatment, no doubt about that. But that doesn't mean she needs to be locked up all her life. But what they did was to perform one of those prefrontal lobotomies on her. You know what that is, do you? Well, that's gone out a long time ago. It never was a successful type of operation and in the past ten years they've been using it less and less. They do that and they can't tell what effect it's going to have on the person. But they did it to her and it made her worse and I want to get her out of there. I promised her I would. Why, I've written her—" he searched through the papers on his desk, picked up one— "I've written eighteen hundred and fifty-one letters without missing a day as of today. And for a while there I used to send her flowers but they put a stop to that."

"How did you send her flowers?"

"Smuggled them out. Only rule I ever broke in here. Bribed the fellow used to drive the state courier truck. He had a regular route; he'd go from here to the hospital and so on. I was growing flowers behind the warden's house and I'd slip the courier a bouquet every day and he'd take them to her. I paid him enough for it. Finally, they found out about it and put a stop to it. You'd think it was a crime to send flowers to somebody.

"But that's the main reason I want to get out, you see. To take care of her. They've turned down my pardon twice now. I don't know why, they won't tell me. One thing they say is, I can't find a job. Well, how can I find a job when I'm in here, I'd like to know? I told them, let me keep the job I've got here now. Half time. Let them pay me whatever it costs the state to have me in here. I'd come here every day and do the same thing I'm doing now. But I'd live outside and I'd look for another job too and I'd be able to take care of Margaret."

He got up, went over to the wall, and took a prison coat from a hook and put it on.

"She's a nice girl," he said. He started to lead the way out into the corridor. Then he stopped and turned back. "Come here," he said. "Look at this."

I followed him into an adjoining cell. On the bed were about fifty Christmas presents, some small and some large, all gaily wrapped in green paper with little gold Santas on it.

The old man picked up one of the larger packages. "Look at that. Heavy. Jars of jelly and jam. I sent to Florida for it. Cost me a dollar and sixty-one cents for air mail postage alone."

He put the present down on the bed and waved his hand over the others. "All for Margaret," he said. "Every one of them."

Then he led the way out of the cell, across the room, and into the corridor. He held out his hand and I took it.

"I've enjoyed talking to you," he said. "Don't get much chance to talk to anybody around here. Well, I've got to go. Come back again some time."

"Good-by," I said.

He went down the corridor, a heavy-set old man with quick eyes who did not want to be late for work.

It may be that without the restraining influence of prison Harold Wesson would aggress in some antisocial way when confronted with an extremely frustrating situation. And if he were pardoned he would encounter many frustrating situations. After over forty years in prison, he would probably find it impossible to adjust to a world in which he has had no experience. This in itself would lead to frustration. Also, he would be unable to obtain Margaret's release from the mental hospital as she is considered definitely psychotic. And there is small possibility that he could find or fit a job other than his present one at the prison. Further, he is at the age where most men retire, not begin a new job. For Wesson, prison is in all probability now a necessary strait jacket against the unleashing of his aggressive emotions, and it is also a cushion against the shocks of the real world. But suppose that a constructive rehabilitation program had been made available to him forty or even thirty years ago. The situation since then might have been quite different. While Wesson has done a great deal for his fellow men, with his extreme intelligence he might have done much more, and been happy as well, had society made opportunity his.

The most significant fact in Harold Wesson's early life which bears on his crime is the extreme degree to which his mother dominated him. She made him do everything as she wished and she insisted that he be with her an abnormal proportion of the time. He was so dependent on her that he never dared to do other than that which she demanded. But acceding to her every demand was necessarily highly frustrating to him time and time again. His own desires went unfulfilled, but he kept the pain of their unfulfillment within him. However, he could not have helped but to have unconsciously developed an enormous resentment, tremendous feelings of aggression, against her. And since she represented all females to him, this submerged aggression generalized, unknown to him, to women as a group.

At the same time, as a developing child, Harold was unable to learn adequately the male role he would later be expected to play. Never allowed to take part in athletics, never allowed to argue or even express his views, he had no opportunity to learn the habits of competitiveness and self-assertiveness demanded of the male by our society. Dominated by his mother and with his father seldom home, he developed as a weak image of his mother: basically feminine, but without her strength of purpose and confidence.

Judging from written reports of those who knew him, Harold was as a young man highly sensitive, seemingly passive: a quiet, nice young man who without being effeminate in the obvious sense was actually more feminine than masculine in his approach to life. As Dr. Taggart, the headmaster at the Greymount School, said: "I think Harold always got along so well with the young ladies on the staff because when he was with them he seemed to forget that he was a man."

But at the same time Harold had a normal sexual urge. This could not be fulfilled because of the dead hand of his mother upon him, saying, in effect, "Sex is not nice. Sex is wrong." Beside this unfulfilled sexual urge, he had that tremendous, submerged aggression against women which was the result of his mother's painful domination of him.

He was, then, a young man in severe conflict: on the one hand, associating with females almost as if he himself were a female; on the other hand, unconsciously both wanting them as sexual partners in order to prove himself a man and hating them for being women.

Then there arose what was for him the extremely frustrating situation of not knowing where he stood with respect to Julia Myers. This it would seem was due largely to the influence of Ruth Johnson. Although it cannot be verified, it would seem that Ruth Johnson had a strong if latent homosexual attachment for Julia Myers. Ruth Johnson recognized Harold as a threat and so she did what she could to place a barrier between him and Julia Myers.

Ruth Johnson thus became Harold's enemy and the focal point of his unconscious aggression toward women. He had been fighting to play his masculine role in society by associating steadily with Julia Myers. And Ruth Johnson kept throwing blocks in the way of this attempt of his to prove himself a man.

At the same time, Harold was also unconsciously aggressive toward Julia Myers. She was a woman and all women were associated with his frustrating mother. Beyond that, Julia Myers had at times indicated a natural enough desire to engage in some degree of physical intimacy. This threw Harold into a specific dilemma: his natural desires and his need to play the masculine role pulling him one way, his mother-induced fear of the immorality of such behavior pulling him in the other direction.

When Ruth Johnson bit Harold's finger and implied that he was making sexual advances toward her, she triggered off all this mounting aggression. The sudden pain of the bitten finger, caused by a woman, and the accusation that he was attempting to do what he really wanted to do—make a sexual advance toward a woman—and yet was afraid to do, were too much for him when coupled with the fact that he saw Ruth Johnson as the frustrater of his relationship with Julia Myers. He lashed out at her and once he began feeling the release of aggression he could not stop himself. Then he went on to rape Julia Myers in a blind attempt to both prove himself a man and to release further his aggression against all women.

But there still remains the question: why did Harold Wesson lose all control of himself on that fateful day? There are many men who have been dominated by their mothers and who as a consequence have been thrown into conflict in their relationships with women and who also are suddenly frustrated by some one woman as Harold was by Ruth Johnson. Yet these men do not necessarily commit murder and rape. Relevant to this question, there are two facts peculiar to Harold's case. First, he had not been able to employ effective socially acceptable or semiacceptable aggression outlets. Second, he had not developed a strong conscience.

With respect to lack of aggression outlets, Harold had been forced by his mother to learn avoidance of these. The usual forms of aggression release—athletics, arguing, sexual behavior, and the like—were tabooed for him by his mother under threat of withdrawal of her love. Thus the aggression mounted within him. Clearly, Harold Wesson is a primary example of an individual whose aggression release was largely compressed into violent outlet on one occasion.

Consider now the second factor peculiar to Harold's case: conscience. Conscience is really a learned set of more or less unconscious fears about what will happen if one commits a socially unacceptable act. If these fears are strong enough, they act as automatic regulators of our behavior. Harold had a conscience, to be sure, but he did not have one which was strong enough to inhibit his enormous aggression when he was confronted with a greatly frustrating situation.

It would seem logical to think that in Harold's case his conscience would be, if anything, overly strong because of his dominating, highly moral mother. But the point here is this: if a parent is too dominating, too militantly moral, the child inwardly rebels. He appears to learn what the parent teaches him; he appears to be docile, co-operative, strong in moral conscience. However, this is on the surface. Underneath there is a strong spark of resentment, kindled over the years by the frustration caused by the parent's excessive demands. The child learns, that is, a surface conscience. But at the core of his being there remains a hidden lawless approach to the world. He never truly internalizes the hated parent's teachings. If he is later confronted with extreme pressure, his surface conscience cracks and his inner attitude of resentful lawlessness drives the compressed aggression outward in one tremendous surge.

6. Prevention and Rehabilitation

T HIS has been an exploratory study into the realm of influences behind murder. Several unavoidable methodological drawbacks are contained in the study. The sample of murderers is probably far from one which is representative of murderers in the United States. Most of the data are drawn from statements made by the mothers about the murderers and control brothers. And it cannot be denied that the mothers' responses may have distorted what actually happened during the early lives of the sons.

Nevertheless, much valuable information has been obtained. On the one hand, the relationships found between frustration or aggression release and murder can serve as rough maps, the accuracy of which may be tested by further research employing finer research tools. On the other hand, there is presented here a detailed objective account of what fifty-one mothers *said* about the early life experiences of their murderer and nonmurderer sons.

But what, in brief, were the major findings of the research reported here and what are the main themes that run through those findings?

First, the murderers as a group were far from being professional killers. Most had murdered during situations in which they were severely upset emotionally. However, it would seem that the learning of the drives which motivated them to kill at those times took place in childhood.

Second, the murderers developed in lower social class environments. By and large, they had learned lower-class subcultures. Educationally and occupationally the murderers achieved little. At the same time, they seem to have had strong desires to rise in the social class hierarchies of their communities.

Third, the mothers of the murderers tended to be women greatly displeased with their social situations. They were, in many instances, highly repressed about sexual and aggressive matters. In sum, I would say that the mothers were well-meaning, maladjusted individuals.

Fourth, and basing this statement largely on the mothers' responses during the interviews, the murderers as a group experienced in infancy and childhood physical frustrations that far outweighed those which the control brothers experienced.

Fifth, a significantly larger number of murderers than of control brothers appear to have been subjected to various psychological frustrations during the preadult years. When the individual murderers' scores on indices of physical and of psychological frustrations were combined, and when the same was done for the individual brothers, it was found that a great majority of the murderers had higher scores than their respective brothers.

Sixth, indices were developed which gave measures of the extents to which the murderers and control brothers made use of socially acceptable and of socially unacceptable aggression releases during their preadult years. A significantly greater number of murderers than of brothers had low scores on the Index of Acceptable Aggression Release. Conversely, a significantly greater number of murderers than of brothers had high scores on the Index of Unacceptable Aggression Release. However, when the scores on these two indices were combined for individual murderers and for individual brothers, there was not a significant difference in the number of murderers and brothers who had low or high scores. As groups, the murderers tended to have used aggression releases about as much as did the brothers. The mean score for the brothers was only slightly higher than for the murderers.

Seventh, the associations between frustration and presence or absence of murder were analyzed by usage of general aggression releases. When aggression release scores were low, both murderers' and control brothers' scores on the Index of General Frustration tended to be somewhat low. Still, the scores for the murderer group were considerably higher than for the control group. However, when aggression release scores were high, the scores for the murderer group on the Index of General Frustration were by and large very high while the scores for the control brothers remained low. Thus, when there was apparently much aggression release in childhood and adolescence, frustration was very strongly associated with murder. When there was little aggression release, frustration was also associated with murder but less strongly.

As I have said, the study reported here is an exploratory one where the roughest of research tools were used. But if those tools have none the less mined ore which contains knowledge about the influences behind murder, then what does that knowledge lead to in terms of prevention of murder? And, if the knowledge is valid with respect to murder, it is probably, although not certainly, applicable to other types of aggressive crime.

Two steps would need to be taken to prevent murder. First, decrease the frustration experienced by individuals in early life. I do not suggest an attempt to reach a zero frustration point. Some frustration is of course necessary for later adjustment to a world which is at times extremely frustrating. But in any case there is small danger of too little frustration. We could, however, concern ourselves with minimizing the terrible physical and psychological frustrations to which a minority of individuals in our society are subjected.

The second step would be to provide more socially acceptable outlets for aggressive feelings. Related to this would be the training of children so that they recognize these outlets and are not fearful of using them.

How might these steps be effected? At three levels: education of future parents; counseling for present parents and their young children; and therapy for adolescents who have already been severely frustrated. The first, educating future parents, is the longest range approach and, I think, the one most likely to produce results.

In what ways can future parents be educated and about what? Beginning in the later grammar school years and continuing through high school, children could be taught the fundamentals of psychology and sociology. This knowledge would lead them better to understand themselves and the children they will eventually train. It would lead them to understand the tremendous influence social relationships and resultant unconscious motivations have on behavior. And such knowledge would allow these future parents to realize the nature and consequence of undue frustration and blocked aggression outlets. To take a specific example: a mother so educated and about to toilet train her child early, abruptly, and frustratingly would be able to look into herself and to see whether her real motivations were to impress others and to work off her own aggression on the child.

Most people in our society never receive training in the behavioral sciences. Consequently they never understand behavior. True, there are human relations courses in some high schools, and psychology and sociology are elective to college students. But the high school courses usually do not deal with the basic principles of psychology and sociology; as for the college courses, most people do not attend college.

I am aware that there is great resistance to the idea of teaching this type of subject matter in grammar and high schools: "It will confuse children." "It goes against American ideals." "Psychology and sociology are only common sense, anyway." "Children can't understand such things."

These are rationalizations adults use to avoid the objective reasons for their actions. Psychology and sociology will tell them what they do not want to hear. And those subjects may, in effect, tell their children what they do not want their children to hear about them, the parents.

Many of the concepts and principles of psychology and sociology could be readily comprehended by twelve- and thirteen-year-olds. It is the adults who have had time to build emotional defenses who find these areas of knowledge difficult to understand. I am not advocating that we turn grammar and high school curricula into behavioral science curricula. But I am suggesting the possibility of equal time for psychology and sociology, time equal to that spent on physical education, cooking, or automobile driving instruction.

I predict that the day will come when behavioral science is taught as a matter of course in the lower schools. But that day is probably a long way off. When it arrives, individuals in our society will live more adjustively, and a long step will have been taken toward solving human problems other than murder.

At a second level of prevention parents and their young children might be provided with counseling, especially with respect to frustration and aggression. However, I doubt that in practice this would work very well. It would be exceedingly difficult and costly to determine which parents and young children most needed the counseling. Further, most parents who needed counseling probably would not make use of it if it were offered to them.

The third level of prevention, therapy for adolescents who have already been severely frustrated, has more practicability than the second. Adolescents in high school who have great amounts of pent-up aggression could be discovered by use in the schools of psychological projective tests. Once discovered, these adolescents could be provided with therapy by the state. The therapy, while taking into account the total personality and environment of the individual, would be focused on opening up for the adolescent acceptable channels of aggression release and on reducing the frustration level of his current circumstances.

Consider now the problem of rehabilitation of convicted murderers. This involves the question of capital punishment; you cannot rehabilitate a dead man. Whether to use capital punishment depends on the goal desired. If the goal is to decrease murder, then it would appear foolish to use capital punishment. A number of studies have shown that when the death penalty is discarded, known homicide does not increase; and when the death penalty is instituted or reinstituted, known homicide does not decrease.[1]

Capital punishment probably does not lead to a decrease in known murder because it is not based on psychologically sound principles. People about to commit murder do not rationally weigh the act against the penalty.[2] On the other hand, some individuals have unconscious drives to place themselves in positions where they will be punished with utmost severity.[3]

My feeling is that the major reason for existence of the death penalty is that it allows the more or less law-abiding members of society one violent aggression outlet. The murderers are, in part at least, the products of the society, and they become its scapegoats.[4]

Another important matter related to the use of the death penalty is this: a number of studies have indicated that about 10 per cent of individuals in selected groups who were executed or imprisoned for life were later found to have been innocent.[5] In all likelihood other individuals in these groups were also innocent, but the facts to indicate such were never uncovered. That 10 or more per cent were not guilty seems to me adequate grounds for abolishing the death penalty.

But in any case assume that the death penalty is not used. Assume that the murderer is incarcerated for some long period. What then of rehabilitation? At present, most prisons in the United States do not have anything approaching adequate rehabilitation programs. They may have them on paper but they do not have them in practice.

What are the criteria for an effective rehabilitation program for individuals convicted of murder? First, the program should be constructed with the realization that the individual must rehabilitate himself but that he must also have competent aid and facilities. That is, he must have as guides people trained in psychology and sociology; he must have an adequate use of language; and he must have up-to-date books.

The second criterion is that those in charge of the program realize that rehabilitation does not consist solely of attempting to aid the individual in changing some of the attitudes basic to his personality structure. Rehabilitation also involves the changing of the individual's group relationships. Personality attitudes and group relationships have reciprocal influences. To build a rehabilitation program around only one of the two means failure. Therefore, while incarcerated the individual must have people around him—other inmates and correctional personnel—who have personalities conducive to social relationships which are rewarding to him and of the kinds approved by the values of the society.

The third criterion is that there must be short-range and long-range meaningful rewards for the individual undergoing rehabilitation. Rehabilitation is fundamentally a learning process. And learning is most efficiently accomplished if rewarded. Short-range rewards might include, for example, work positions of increased responsibility and prestige within the institution. Long-range rewards would include the clear opportunity for the individual to take up one day a more or less prestigeful life in the general society unmarred by the stigmas that now result from imprisonment.

The three above criteria apply to the rehabilitation not only of murderers but of criminals in general. Therefore, what further criteria might be used for a program of rehabilitation for murderers specifically? If the study reported here has validity, then a fourth criterion is that the individual could be guided in such a way that he comes to see what were the impersonal events and the personal circumstances, the latter arising out of past group relationships, that led to a build-up of aggression within him.

Fifth, through therapy, the individual could be brought to perceive how and why he was unable to make use of acceptable aggression outlets and how he can do so in the future.

Sixth, group therapy for murderers could be employed. This would make possible situations in which they would have opportunities both to work out their guilt feelings and practice using acceptable aggression outlets.

A further suggestion is that individuals who were convicted of murder or other felonies and have been released from prison form a national Criminals Anonymous. Foolish? Impossible? I don't think so. What person convicted of a serious crime and later released would want to go around advertising his crime? Many, I think. I believe that part of the success of Alcoholics Anonymous is that it allows the individual to work off some of his guilt feelings by saying, in effect, "I was an alcoholic." I believe the same mechanism would operate in the cases of many nonprofessional criminals.

True, paroled or conditionally pardoned felons generally are forbidden by law to associate with known felons. These laws can be modified. Most nonprofessional criminals, murderers especially, are not the type who get together with other criminals to plot further crimes.

Criminals Anonymous could operate in and out of prisons. It could lend psychological support to criminals incarcerated as well as those released. And it would be a great aid in establishing normal social relationships for the individual. The fact that the members of Criminals Anonymous would be individuals convicted of murder and other serious felonies in no way means that they could not supply normal social relationships. Criminals eat, drink, love, worry, work as do other human beings. And generally they obey the law, as do other human beings.

I would suggest, however, that a Criminals Anonymous group not divorce itself from behavioral science to the extent Alcoholics Anonymous has. True, Alcoholics Anonymous has worked well because of the support it supplies alcoholics. But I suspect it would have had even greater success if there had been more recognition of the value of a knowledge of psychology and sociology.

Above and beyond everything said here, we should attempt to realize that murderers, and most if not all other criminals, are largely products of their culture and of their interactions with other people. This cultural and social experience determines in great part the unconscious drives of the individual's personality. If that experience is adverse, those unconscious drives are likely to result in seriously negative behavior. In this sense, we must all share in the responsibility for each crime. For we all contribute to our culture in one way or another. And we all interact with others and so help to shape them as they do us. Where we fail most, I think, is in our general refusal to press forward rapidly toward a clear, objective understanding of human behavior.

The Views of Joseph T. Galvin

WITH the close association I have had over the past fourteen years with all types of people convicted of murder, it is possible that I may have information that might throw some light on the question of the influences behind murder.

I believe it was your idea, Dr. Palmer, that a key to most murders might be located somewhere in the infancy or childhood of the convicted person; that a frustration or a series of frustrations, connected or single instances, might be a major cause of this crime. I can go along with this credo to a certain point, then I must walk in another direction. I believe that where the murderer is of a borderline intelligence or emotionally unstable personality, it is very possible that frustration in infancy will leave an indelible mark on the person. But what of the paid professional killer? Still, to be utterly fair, the mercenary may be fulfilling a power lack caused by some set of circumstances in childhood; thus compensating in mature life with the crime of killing; thus obtaining the gratification he lacked in childhood. Most of the few paid killers I knew were physically weak. That may mean something.

Economic factors in murder? My experience tells me that they bear little or no weight in most cases. Possibly economy, perhaps unrealized, is a factor in abortions of certain kinds. I believe that any taking of life, save that in self-defense, is murder, regardless of who performs the deed. Perhaps I am prejudiced in this respect.

Passion killings do illustrate perhaps most of all your idea that frustration may play an important part in murder. Love unrequited can be a most dangerous state. Love scorned also is a major cause in bringing many men to this prison; in fact most of the men here who have been convicted of murder are either wife or sweetheart slayers, sad as it may be.

Oscar Wilde said it nicely: "Each man kills the thing he loves . . ." and so it seems here also.

Alcohol and its abuse has also its share of victims so far as murder is concerned. Alcoholism, as you know, according to some people, is merely a return to the oral erotic stage. And if that is not an infantile state with all its frustrations, then what is?

I have read and heard it said that people who commit murder are not normal. For if they were, everyone would be committing murder and then it would no longer be considered a crime. Somehow I believe myself that most crimes of murder are the result of maladjustment to the calls of our immediate society. The individual lacks the ability to react immediately in a normal way to an abnormal situation. He or she sheds the veneer of civilization and acts as a primordial animal. Inherently, we are all capable of killing if the circumstances are extreme enough to demand this of us. Some of us retain the safeguard of civilization and custom and just yell at our wives or kick the cat. Some of us don't. The latter are the ones that come to prison labeled as killers.

How does a man convicted of murder feel? Being a convicted man, I can say without a reservation of any nature that I am only too well aware of how he is treated and how he must feel. I lived it.

I believe it takes approximately three years before a man actually realizes what he has done. Most of the men that I have been close to tell that they did not truly realize where they were until a period roughly of three years had passed. It may be a defense mechanism the mind sets up, but it is definitely there. Many men are remorseful and many claim they just don't feel anything at all. Many men say that were the circumstances the same, they would act accordingly again.

You ask if it really takes three years before a man realizes that he is in for life, and that he is, before the law, a convicted slayer? I have spoken just recently to twenty-five men on this very thing within the past few days, and all say the same. This number is approximately one-quarter of the lifers in this institution. Some of the men I spoke to said that the first few years were dream-world stuff—that this really wasn't happening to them and that they would soon wake up in their own homes. These men are neither cretins nor morons but just confused men who never realized exactly what had happened. Defense mechanism?

Other men constantly think over the trial: Where did the law triumph? How can they do this? Will I get a new trial? These men refuse to face the fact that they are lifers. When after a period of three years has passed and they are still confined, they begin to understand that they are in prison, not for a few weeks or a few years, but for the rest of their natural lives. Then the separation of the men from the boys commences. Some of these men accept the new order and become model prisoners; the biggest majority are in this category. They are good workers and soon establish a fine record for both work and deportment. These men are truly not criminals, but lawbreakers.

On the other hand, you have the men who cannot adjust to this new and bitter existence. These men, thank God, are few in numbers. They refuse to take part in the new social life. They remain aloof from the majority of the prisoners. They create new worlds of their own and nothing cruel or bitter for themselves can enter. They usually wind up in the psycho ward. A very few try suicide, and fewer succeed. I personally think that it is merely a bid for sympathy.

But to return to how the convicted slayer feels. Fundamentally, each man is an individual case and must be viewed thusly. There truly is no rule that applies to all. One man that I know well went out to hold up a gasoline station. He completed the robbery and was backing out the door when he tripped and fell. The gun went off and the robbery victim became a murder victim. The slayer said he was sorry but that "it was just one of those things." I think this man is only sorry that he was caught, and not through genuine remorse. His every action and gesture belie any real sorrow.

Across the hall from this man is another youth who committed a shocking killing of a near blood relative. It was so atrocious a crime that this man was sentenced to death. He later was committed for life. This second man claims he has absolutely no recollection of what occurred during the time of the crime. Still, he is remorseful and sorry, and says, "If I did do this thing, though I cannot remember, I would cheerfully give my life to bring her back to life."

Slayer number two is quiet and courteous to all, prefers the solitude of his room too much; whereas slayer number one must always be with someone. Why? Afraid of his thoughts? Slayer number two was in prison a little over three years before he opened a book or wrote a letter. He had retreated into a sphere where nothing bad ever happened. His bubble broke when he was transferred here from the old Charlestown prison. He has made a satisfactory adjustment now and will or should continue. Slayer number one will never adjust until he becomes honest with himself.

I sincerely do not believe that capital punishment will ever have any deterring effect on murder. In very, very few cases does a person ever coldly plan a murder, weighing his chances of being caught. Thus the deterring value of losing his own life does not play any part. Most of the murders committed are spur-of-the-moment tragedies. Life imprisonment as it is today is merely long-drawn-out murder. It definitely is not the answer. I think that *imprisonment with the definite view of rehabilitation and education of the man* is the answer. Many men find themselves in prison, but their keen intellects are forever debarred from the public good because of a moment of passion. If a man is confined one day to life, and there is a definite effort made by the authorities to aid this person, within a few years in most cases a decent valuable citizen can be returned to the society that needs him. However, you know and I know that this truth will not be recognized by the public for many years to come. I hope that I live to see it, Dr. Palmer.

One odd fact looms up, and it is this: very few lifers in this state of Massachusetts try to escape. Perhaps there is an unconscious wish for punishment—and the good Lord knows that life in prison is atonement for any crime. The majority of lifers in this prison were all good family men, men with church records behind them. Yet, for one moment of madness, they must remain behind these walls until either death or a merciful governor frees them. Almost any of these men could be released from prison within one day to one year, and never commit another antisocial act during the remainder of their lives. Society refuses to believe this truth. Perhaps one day society will recognize this fact, and do something about it.

What are the best methods for aiding murderers to rehabilitate themselves? This is a question that I have taken all through the entire camp to the men most concerned with this problem, the convicted men. All agree that the first step must be taken by the man himself. But to take this step he must have hope. That is the most important thing in this place or any other of its nature. Man without hope is dead. Rehabilitate, according to Webster's first definition, means to restore to a former capacity. Now, while the man is in prison that obviously is an impossibility, so we must take the next best thing. We are prisoners of the state, of society; we are not free. Our whole life and habits must be built or predicated on that fact. It is evident that our way of thought was wrong, else we should not be here. So we must change our manner of cogitation.

In prison, our lives are so regimented that we scarcely have to think for ourselves. We are told when to eat, when to sleep, when to work, and when to play. We are advised how to write, whom to associate with. The simple mechanics of living are disposed of; but what of our thoughts? This is where the true beginnings of rehabilitation start.

Honesty with yourself is a must, for if you can't be honest with you, who can you be honest with? Most people realize this here and act accordingly. Some of our men find the start of the road in the church; others find it in painstaking work, where an error shows glaringly. Others like myself find it in social reconstruction in Alcoholics Anonymous. When you look at things honestly, you almost always see them in an entirely different light, and they look better.

The next important thing to try to impress upon the men

is that, though we are prisoners, we are prisoners only in body, that our minds are as free as we permit them to be. Mix with the other men, see how they think, discuss your case as far as you feel free to do so. The vast majority of us convicted men will only be given one chance to make good via parole, so it is up to us to be as ready for street and for society as we can make ourselves. *If we can prove to ourselves that the entire world is not against us*, then the big step to reclamation is taken successfully.

A lifer in an average prison is usually given a position of trust, and ninety-nine times out of a hundred he will never violate a trust. Any warden or superintendent will back up that statement. If the newspapers would only try to give the lifer a break, and not crucify him for his efforts, another huge step would have been taken. But somehow the papers can only scream, "Murder most foul." You must give the man hope of ultimate release before any tangible improvement can be noted or even thought of. Once the public and the papers realize that, then another forward step has been taken. If the same amount of publicity were given to all the men who make good as is given the tiny fraction of the whole that fail, still another step forward would result.

Education in prison can mean many things—not only those that are to be learned from schoolbooks. However, we are concerned with bettering our ways, and experience has proved that books are about the best way. We have so much time to utilize in some way that we can do little better than to pick up those books and study.

Further, I firmly believe that a modern system of teaching trades in these places of confinement can aid a great deal. Far too many prisons still have men doing obsolete types of manufacture. A prime, in fact a most necessary and vital, factor which relates to all phases of prison life is this: all new inmates should be given aptitude tests. There are far too many cases of round pegs in square openings. I have seen men who were qualified in their respective fields shunted indifferently and at times foolishly into jobs that were so far from their abilities that it was sheer wasted manpower, not to mention broken tools and wasted materials. It is a recognized fact that many men entering prisons are not noted for their mental acuity. But it is a sad fact that there is a great tendency on the part of various institutions to regard all prisoners as being of low mental age and ability. If a man is fitted to the job, then put him on it; do not try to fit the man to the job, regardless of his innate ability. A man will try harder at a job he is familiar with than one about which he is ignorant.

What is my opinion of a project similar to Alcoholics Anonymous for convicted men? In several states and in Canada there are already groups very close to that idea, and they seem to be functioning well. In Massachusetts and many states, such a group would be an infraction of the law. "Consorting with a known criminal" is against the law, and it is sufficient to send a man back to prison, especially if he is on parole. The idea in itself is excellent, but one that must be approached with caution and care.

Here is one other argument against a Criminals Anonymous. Alcoholics Anonymous starts with honesty and all its functions work out from that focal point. In the case of a C.A., would a professional or a pathological thief have a chance of making the program work? In A.A. we have many members who are doing time for larceny, but 99 per cent only stole when they were either drunk, getting drunk, or pathologically intoxicated. How about C.A. members? Most pro thieves won't take a drink or a drunk on a job! I really believe that if a man could influence his fellows sufficiently, C.A. would work, perhaps only with the minor offenders, but even then what matter? Were only one man to change his illegal ways, C.A. would be a truly worth-while success.

In California there is preparole school where a parolee who has made good comes back to the prison to talk to the men who are to be released in the near future. This seems to work out well for the new men, but, according to what I read in penal press, the recidivists heed not a word. Perhaps one day we may be able to get a penological Billy Graham who may be the influence we need to make a program of this nature feasible.

One thing I would like to make clear: despite what newspapers say to the contrary, most old-timers who are doing time do not pervert or exert a bad influence on the young inmate. Many go far out of their way to befriend and help a new man. Occasionally we do have a "wolf," as an old pervert is termed, who tries to catch a new man in his net. But this happens far less than the public believes. Most of the time it is more of a case of a young pervert being found out rather than an older man influencing the youth. This situation is not confined to prisons, as you know. It exists wherever men, and women too, are forced to live an unnatural life; by that I mean a life without normal gratification of sexual desires. Everyone cannot sublimate his desires.

Upon entry to a prison the lifer should be given a thorough examination by a team of competent psychiatrists and sociologists, a recheck every six months for the first three years, then a yearly progress check. I think that many men could be salvaged from their wrecked lives. I would make school compulsory for all whom the doctors deemed mentally capable of learning. A proper job placement bureau is a must. Too many men sit in wasteful idleness for too many years. This is wasteful to the state and disastrous to the man himself.

I heartily endorse the "day to life" for all lifers, with honest examinations every three years and the hope of ultimate freedom. Here in New England the average lifer serves an average of twenty-eight years before he is freed on parole, a broken old man who in most cases is a charge of either the public or his folks. In either case he is a liability and can never be an asset again. This is revenge, not rehabilitation, and you can't have both in modern penology.

Through the above mentioned approaches, the imbeciles and morons could be weeded out, as could the so-called psychopathic killers and the amoral mercenary slayers. *Most* lifers are lawbreakers, not criminals.

An enlightened public press is a lovely dream but I am afraid we will never see it. Too many men are tried and convicted before they even see a courtroom—all because of the press. I would have all people who are connected with the prisoners in any way at all educated and paid enough so that they would be out of reach of all newspaper and political pressure.

A sensible supervised parole system is a must, so that each parolee does not merely check in and say he is working and behaving himself. The parole system must give the released lifer a place where he can bring his problems for possible solution.

All this spells hope for the lifer, and he needs that to live, just as you do. Regardless of the fact that we are in prison, it would be well for the world to remember these words: "But for the grace of God, there go I."

The Views of Raymond V. Peters

TO ME, the definition of the term "rehabilitate" that is most applicable to penal inmates, particularly to those who have been convicted of homicide, is "to regenerate, or make over in an improved form." It means making of oneself a confident human being able to cope with and adjust to the ever changing order of society. It means not only acquiring sense but the exercise of sense in order to make that sense grow. In short, rehabilitation is the realization and acceptance that life is a combination of freedom and the voluntary or forced restraint of freedom; rehabilitation is the recognition of the difference between the restrictions that have to be self-imposed and those that are imposed from without; and rehabilitation is the learning of self-discipline and restraint.

Over a period of some twenty-five years of confinement, I have found that most of the penal inmates with whom I have come in contact, and particularly those who had served "time" previous to a conviction for homicide, seemed to reason that "rehabilitation" is something that one just picks out of the air; that it should come automatically, if enough of it is present in the atmosphere of a penal institution to rub off on them; that it is a sort of tangible something that one need simply be exposed to. A common gripe heard was: "Rehabilitation, baloney!" (Or a more pungent term.) "What are they doing to rehabilitate me?"

The lack of understanding that the individual must rehabilitate himself was prevalent. The recognition that "they" can only *offer* rehabilitative opportunities and that the opportunities must be *sought* had only penetrated to a few, for it is difficult to reason out such problems when the intrinsic values in prison and those outside are so far separated. How does this recognition arrive? How does one help to change the thinking of penal inmates who, as a result of their acts, face long years of confinement? How does one try to explain the satisfactions that may be derived from co-operative and harmonious living on the "outside," or even the "inside," to a "lifer"? How does one set into motion a program that will help change the thinking of a man who is vengeful, embittered, and a product of a life where there has been a lack of understanding, of initiative, of love?

Men who have been convicted of homicide and sentenced to be confined to a penal institution for a long term of years, or the "remainder of their natural lives," do not bring with them into prison any real hope of profiting by this experience. Each one enters prison with a different set of emotions; some with bravado and vengefulness; some with guilt and fear; still others with remorse; a few with an acceptance of their situation and a willingness to search for the reasons that led to their confinement. To each, however, irrespective of personal emotions, there is nothing more important than what is going to happen in their immediate future. "Hope," in one form or another, is ever present. There are few, indeed, who will not admit to themselves that one day they will be "on the street" again. How the goal will be attained may be vague and hazy, interspersed with fanciful thinking, but the need as well as the hope is present. The period just after entering prison is the one time when the defenses are just below the surface; when the full import of what has happened occupies the mind. It is the period when the inmate is more receptive to genuine understanding than he may ever again be during his confinement. It is the time when understanding can be more important than a wide knowledge of devices for influencing others. It is the time to begin the regeneration and the making over in a new form. It cannot be delayed; that is, it cannot be delayed if the average inmate's concept of a penal institution as a place of punishment is to be changed.

Statistically, it is true that more than 90 per cent of all persons convicted of homicide, who receive terms of penal confinement, are eventually granted their freedom by means of parole, pardon, or executive clemency. In the light of this, it is more than important that classification of the inmate be complete: his needs assessed, his personal interests plumbed, his training program geared to a field in which he will be most likely to succeed, a program devised that will hold his interest and merit his co-operation.

It is my thesis that the main purposes of a constructive rehabilitative program should be to (1) help the inmate to build a sense of responsibility; (2) teach him how best to become economically sufficient; (3) explain to him, in nontechnical terms, the difference between internal desires and external reality; and (4) help him to supply his needs emotionally.

No man lives in a vacuum, not even a "lifer." Despite his wishful belief in his eventual freedom, he feels the haunting fear that he has been consigned to spend the remainder of his life doing the same things over and over, subject to the whims and caprices of those who watch over him. Fears live and grow in isolation and they find fertile soil in the mind of the individual who feels he does not belong. And although he has been segregated from society, the long-termer still retains his basic trait of human nature: the yearning to belong. Man, by his very nature, must have a purpose in life, an attainable and satisfying purpose. No matter what his mentality it must be put to some worthy use or that mentality's presence alone can serve to destroy him. How best can he be taught that he does belong, that although society has banished him it is willing to adopt an objective attitude toward him, if he is willing to try to rehabilitate himself?

In order to secure and hold the co-operation of the inmate, he must first be helped to build a sense of responsibility. This is possible with a program of social education which has body enough to impress upon him the satisfactions that may be derived from co-operative and harmonious living. This program must help to provide an opportunity to develop more understanding of other people, why they behave as they do and how it is possible to adjust to them. Such a program of social education should include lectures by judges, police officials, community officials, educators, and businessmen. The lectures should be followed by question-and-answer periods that help to promote understanding by both the inmate and society. It would seem to follow that each speaker should be sympathetic to the philosophy of rehabilitation.

Most inmates when assigned to work are not, unfortunately, placed at a task which they like or may learn to like. They should be assigned to work tasks according to capabilities, interests, physical abilities, and all other factors necessary for consideration in a training program. There should be a specific trade as an interest center, in keeping with an inmate's capacities. Then, and only then, can a background be developed around it. In full, it should be the purpose of all connected with a rehabilitation program to equip the inmate so that he may become a producing social asset. While learning to make auto tags, cement pipe, brooms, and things of a like nature is helpful in maintaining a state's budget, they are not marketable trades. In this sense, when an inmate gripes, "What are they doing to rehabilitate me?" he strikes a bell note.

Employment following release from prison, even if it is considered to be in the distant future, should be a factor in both work assignment and academic interests, or little can be gained. There should be an employment placement program, or all the training will not mean a thing if the inmate is eventually released to a job he has neither a liking nor an aptitude for. Even if an institution is not set up for teaching marketable trades, to initiate the program there could be opportunities for selected inmates to learn the practical sides of baking, cooking, kitchen management, purchasing, bookkeeping, machine operation, lathe operation, plumbing, pipe-fitting, as well as many others in the maintenance field. There could be split shifts for work assignment, job training, and classroom study. It is, of course, true that all inmates cannot reach the same level. Yet, is it not possible to train those with a limited capacity in a variety of occupations and help to enlarge their employability range?

An inmate's attitude is much influenced by those who supervise his work. If it is mostly, "You do what we tell you to do. We'll do the thinking," the inmate's attitude is influenced in the wrong direction. If one does not think, one cannot advance no matter how hard he tries. The inmate must be taught more than the habitual reaction to a working situation. The approach should be one that will help him to delve further into the workability of any idea he may have. He should be permitted to pursue his idea to see if he can substantiate what he says. If he cannot, just as much is gained, for he will then see for himself why this or that works better in its present form. However, if his new approach is helpful, the inmate will try to think of other problems as well. As a result, he will begin to gain in his quest for rehabilitation, even though he may not at first recognize it.

W. A. White has suggested that "the criminal is the scapegoat of the public conscience." Since he made that statement some forty-odd years ago, the community's predominant concept of the prison as a place of punishment has changed very little. This is one of the reasons why crime continues to grow instead of decrease, why there are more crimes of violence and more recidivists. The community cannot adopt the attitude that it is possible to rehabilitate and punish at the same time, or believe that retribution must be "complete" before a man is rehabilitated, and hope to see lasting results. Yet this attitude is one of the reasons why most persons employed in a prison program are not competent and sympathetic to the philosophy of rehabilitation. If men employed by penal institutions were made to feel that they were a part of the job of helping to remake prisoners, it would lend importance and dignity to their position. It would help them to see the philosophy of rehabilitation in a different light. When the theme is, "You're here to be punished and we're here to punish you," the philosophy of rehabilitation is dealt a body blow.

All murderers seem to be, at the time of their act or during the events leading to it, moved by emotions they have neither the knowledge nor the insight to understand. The dilemma is that they know of no other way of gaining momentary security except by a method that deprives another of life. The act may be committed during a fit of unreasoning anger, as a result of pent-up emotions. It may be the result of a long-thought-out plan; the panic of fear of one's own safety during a robbery; or a sadistic desire to kill in a mind that never developed beyond the law of the jungle. It may be because of an animus toward authority engendered both with or without reason. Whatever the cause, the murderer never asks himself, "Am I willing to pay the price of me?" And he never says to himself, "The price I pay for committing this act is me."

Why do murderers act as they do? And what can be done to help them recognize the difference between the restrictions that have to be self-imposed and those that are imposed from without, and to learn self-discipline and restraint? Generally speaking, we usually understand our own motives as vaguely as we understand the reasons for the behavior of others. Too often the reasons we assign for our own are incorrect or partial explanations. Internal desires and external reality are terms that most murderers don't comprehend even though they may be aware of the definitions. Each person is being affected continually by external circumstances and, no matter how well we may understand a murderer's organization and his way of acting, such influences are vital elements in his conduct. All of us who have been convicted of murder, and many of those who have not, have refused to be swayed by external reality, by the price that has to be paid. I do not refer to the act of murder itself, of which there may be many degrees, but to the lack of the learning of self-discipline and restraint that led to the act. In this sense, the act is simply a by-product. We who have killed never acquired the devices of thinking or conduct by which the ego suppressed the demand of the id or the self-discipline and restraint that in most people conscience is supposed to provide. Thus we have to be taught, and it is a bit startling to realize that most of the teaching has to come after a conviction for murder.

It is not difficult to explain to a person that the test of anything is its usefulness. It is not difficult to explain that something has developed in human nature which will not permit the jungle law of tooth and claw; that the state, as a representative of the people, has to step in whenever it can promote the general welfare; that as a result the murderer must be banished from society; that he has no survival value. Can it not, then, be explained to any average mind that there is no place for anger in a rational human life; that anger is not inherent in modern human beings; that anger is an animal response rather than a rational human response; that the law of fierceness is the law of the jungle? A man has to see it for himself and be his own judge, but if the differences between internal desires and external reality are explained in nontechnical, everyday language, he will come to see that force has two edges and that the one used against him by society may prove to be sharper than the one he has used.

The desire for esteem is of crucial importance. All of us seek it in one or another of its forms. It is a better incentive than any other psychological reward. It is the keystone of a man's emotional needs. It is what the murderer serving a long term in a penal institution lacks. It may be that his lack of esteem for himself is due to his crime. Or it may be that he sought to acquire it by committing his homicidal act and found it was an empty goal. The desire to be considered important is a powerful motivating force, but one can be important only as long as he supplies needs for others.

In order to help a murderer supply his needs emotionally while he is serving a long term of penal confinement, it is necessary first to help him to acquire a sound set of values, values that only reflective thinking can bring to him. The initial ones would seem to be co-operation and the understanding of co-operative living. Guidance should be completely individual, whenever and wherever possible. It should help to give the inmate insight into his personal problems, teach him to make good use of his leisure time. It should be impressed upon him that making himself into a new form requires positive effort; that needs can only be met by combined efforts; that his approach should be an empirical one wherein he tests and experiments rather than accepts without substantiation. Everyone has an especial interest. Help him to develop it, and his other interests will have a greater chance to grow. In other words, capitalize the assets and supply the deficiencies of the individual. Adjust his goal to his capacities, and, if his sense of reality can be awakened and he is the possessor of normal intelligence and normal mental equipment, he will come to see that the accepted way is probably the best way.

In summation, we say that the murderer's emotional attitude as well as his mental capacities must be considered; that his initiative should be increased and his sense of responsibility broadened; and that while devices for influencing him may work at times, genuine understanding when a critical situation arises should supersede any routine method of influence. It is my belief that genuine understanding helped me to come face to face with what I really was and changed my thinking. This is why I will always believe that it is never too late for any man.

Notes

Chapter 1

1. See annual bulletins of: Federal Bureau of Investigation, *Uniform Crime Reports for the United States* (Washington: U.S. Government Printing Office).
2. First-degree manslaughter is frequently termed nonnegligent manslaughter.
3. Second-degree manslaughter is frequently termed negligent manslaughter.
4. Federal Bureau of Investigation, *Uniform Crime Reports for the United States*, Annual Bulletin for 1957 (Washington: U.S. Government Printing Office), p. 71.
5. U.S. Bureau of the Census, *Statistical Abstract of the United States: 1957* (Washington: U.S. Government Printing Office, 1957), p. 5.
6. Federal Bureau of Investigation, *loc. cit.*
7. *Ibid.*, p. 118.
8. This statement is based on firsthand reports from Icelanders.
9. See annual bulletins of: Federal Bureau of Investigation, *Uniform Crime Reports for the United States* (Washington: U.S. Government Printing Office).
10. *Loc. cit.*
11. *Loc. cit.*
12. E. Frankel, "One Thousand Murderers," *Journal of Criminal*

Law and Criminology, XXIX, No. 5 (1939), pp. 667–688.

13. For example: David Abrahamsen, *Crime and the Human Mind* (New York: Columbia University Press, 1944), ch. 8. Robert Lindner, *The Fifty-Minute Hour* (New York: Rinehart, 1955), ch. 1.

14. For example: John L. Gillin, *The Wisconsin Prisoner* (Madison: University of Wisconsin Press, 1946), ch. 6. Marvin E. Wolfgang, *Patterns in Criminal Homicide* (Philadelphia: University of Pennsylvania Press, 1958).

15. Robert M. Lindner, *Stone Walls and Men* (New York: Odyssey Press, 1946), pp. 97–101.

16. Gillin, *op. cit.*

17. *Ibid.,* p. 86.

18. *Ibid.,* p. 87.

19. For example: H. C. Brearley, *Homicide in the United States* (Chapel Hill: University of North Carolina Press, 1932). John L. Gillin, *op. cit.* Thorsten Sellin, editor, *Murder and the Penalty of Death, Annals of the American Academy of Political and Social Science,* November, 1952.

20. For example: Croswell Bowen, *They Went Wrong* (New York: McGraw-Hill, 1954), ch. 2. Lucy Freeman, *Catch Me Before I Kill More* (New York: Crown, 1955). Richard Gehman, *A Murder in Paradise* (New York: Rinehart, 1954). Robert Lindner, *The Fifty-Minute Hour* (New York: Rinehart, 1955). Maureen McKernan, *The Amazing Crime and Trial of Leopold and Loeb* (New York: The New American Library of World Literature, 1957).

21. John Dollard *et al., Frustration and Aggression* (New Haven: Yale University Press, 1939).

22. For example: Edwin H. Sutherland and Donald R. Cressey, *Principles of Criminology* (Chicago: J. B. Lippincott, 1955), pp. 129, 143.

Chapter 2

1. For example: E. Frankel, "One Thousand Murderers," *Journal of Criminal Law and Criminology,* XXIX, No. 5 (1939), pp. 687–688.

2. *Loc. cit.*

3. U.S. Bureau of the Census, *Statistical Abstract of the United States: 1957* (Washington: U.S. Government Printing Office, 1957), p. 31.
4. The prestige levels of the residential areas were assigned on the basis of the interviewers' judgments.
5. U.S. Bureau of the Census, *op. cit.*, p. 112.
6. For abbreviated statement of the scale, see A. B. Hollingshead and F. C. Redlich, *Social Class and Mental Illness* (New York: John Wiley, 1958), pp. 390–391.
7. For abbreviated statement of the index, see A. B. Hollingshead, R. Ellis, and E. Kirby, "Social Mobility and Mental Illness," *American Sociological Review*, XIX, No. 5, p. 579.
8. A. B. Hollingshead and F. C. Redlich, "Social Stratification and Psychiatric Disorders," *American Sociological Review*, XVIII, No. 1, p. 167. Based on a three-factor index of social position.
9. W. Lloyd Warner and Paul S. Lunt, *The Social Life of a Modern Community* (New Haven: Yale University Press, 1941), p. 376.

Chapter 6

1. Karl F. Schuessler, "The Deterrent Influences of the Death Penalty," *Annals of the American Academy of Political and Social Science*, November, 1952, pp. 54–62. George B. Vold, "Can the Death Penalty Prevent Crime?" *The Prison Journal*, October, 1932, pp. 3–8.
2. Thorsten Sellin, "Common Sense and the Death Penalty," *The Prison Journal*, October, 1932, p. 12.
3. For example: David Abrahamsen, *Crime and the Human Mind* (New York: Columbia University Press, 1944). See also Abrahamsen's *Who Are the Guilty?* (New York: Rinehart, 1952).
4. Franz Alexander and Hugo Staub, *The Criminal, the Judge and the Public, a Psychological Analysis* (London: Allen and Unwin, 1931), pp. 207–225. Robert Kann, "Criminal Law and Aggression," *Psychoanalytic Review*, July, 1941, pp. 384–406.
5. Frank E. Hartung, *On Capital Punishment*, Wayne Univer-

sity Department of Sociology and Anthropology, Detroit, Mich., 1951. Lewis E. Lawes, *Twenty Thousand Years in Sing Sing* (New York: R. Long and R. R. Smith, 1932), pp. 146–147, 156. See also Edwin M. Borchard, *Convicting the Innocent* (New Haven: Yale University Press, 1932).

Appendix A

Table 1

Social Class Position of Fathers of Murderers and of Residents of Two New England Cities

	% of Fathers	% of Residents of New Haven *	% of Residents of Newburyport **
I	2.0	3.1	3.0
II	3.9	8.1	10.3
III	3.9	22.0	28.4
IV	33.3	46.0	32.9
V	53.0	17.8	25.4
Unknown	3.9	3.0	0.0
Total	100.0	100.0	100.0

* Taken from A. B. Hollingshead and F. C. Redlich, "Social Stratification and Psychiatric Disorders," *American Sociological Review*, XVIII, No. 1, p. 167. Based on a three-factor index of social position.

** Revised data from W. Lloyd Warner and Paul S. Lunt, *The Social Life of a Modern Community* (New Haven: Yale University Press, 1941), p. 376.

Table 2
Murderers and Control Brothers Who Associated Predominantly
with Nondelinquent and Delinquent Boys at Age 16

	Number of Murderers	Number of Brothers
Nondelinquents	30	48
Delinquents	14	2
Unknown or Doesn't Apply *	7	1
Total	51	51

$$X^2 = 12.820 \qquad P < 0.01$$

* Not included in X^2 calculation.

Table 3
Extent to Which Murderers and Control Brothers Dated Girls
at about Age 17

	Number of Murderers	Number of Brothers
Once a Week	4	16
Less Than Once a Week	18	20
Never	15	9
Unknown or Doesn't Apply *	14	6
Total	51	51

$$X^2 = 8.092 \qquad P < 0.05$$

* Not included in X^2 calculation.

Table 4
Marital Harmony of Murderers and Control Brothers

	Number of Murderers	Number of Brothers
Harmonious	7	26
Disharmonious	10	4
Unknown *	0	3
Total	17	33

$$X^2 = 10.756 \qquad P < 0.01$$

* Not included in X^2 calculation.

Table 5
*Number of Serious Operations Performed on Murderers and Control Brothers before Age 12 ***

	Number of Murderers	Number of Brothers
Two **	5	0
One **	9	4
None	37	47
Total	51	51

$$X^2 = 6.746 \qquad P < 0.01$$

* In no case were more than two serious operations performed on any one individual.
** Combined for X^2 calculation.

Table 6
Number of Serious Illnesses Experienced by Murderers and
Control Brothers before Age 12

	Number of Murderers	Number of Brothers
Four *	3	0
Three *	4	1
Two *	12	0
One	18	14
None	14	36
Total	51	51

$$X^2 = 26.380 \qquad P < 0.01$$

* Combined for X^2 calculation.

Table 7
Number of Serious Accidents Occurring to Murderers and
Control Brothers before Age 12

	Number of Murderers	Number of Brothers
Three *	1	0
Two *	1	0
One *	18	6
None	31	45
Total	51	51

$$X^2 = 10.116 \qquad P < 0.01$$

* Combined for X^2 calculation.

Table 8
Ages of Murderers and Control Brothers When Mothers
Started Toilet Training

Age in Months	Number of Murderers	Number of Brothers
Under 6 *	6	1
6–11 *	23	17
12–17 **	17	25
18–23 **	2	5
24 of More **	2	2
Unknown ***	1	1
Total	51	51
$X^2 = 4.858$		$P < 0.05$

* Combined for X^2 calculation.   ** Combined for X^2 calculation.
*** Not included in X^2 calculation.

Table 9
Frequency with Which Mothers Were Afraid Murderers and
Control Brothers Would Be Hurt When about Age 5

	Number of Murderers	Number of Brothers
Almost Always *	11	8
Usually *	13	3
About Half the Time	3	8
Occasionally **	6	14
Very Seldom or Never **	17	18
Unknown ***	1	0
Total	51	51
$X^2 = 8.569$		$P < 0.05$

* Combined for X^2 calculation.   ** Combined for X^2 calculation.
*** Not included in X^2 calculation.

Table 10
*Extent to Which Murderers and Control Brothers Liked
First 4 Years of Grammar School*

	Number of Murderers	Number of Brothers
Liked	23	37
Neutral	5	9
Disliked	23	5
Total	$\overline{51}$	$\overline{51}$

$$X^2 = 15.980 \qquad P < 0.01$$

Table 11
*Frequency with Which Murderers and Control Brothers Became
Emotionally Upset at about Age 5 (Excluding Anger and
Temper Tantrums)*

	Number of Murderers	Number of Brothers
Once a Day *	7	0
Once a Week *	13	0
Once a Month **	1	3
Once Every 6 Months **	1	11
Once a Year **	0	4
Less Than Once a Year ** (But at Least Once)	0	1
Never	28	31
Unknown ***	1	1
Total	$\overline{51}$	$\overline{51}$

$$X^2 = 33.914 \qquad P < 0.01$$

* Combined for X^2 calculation.
** Combined for X^2 calculation.
*** Not included in X^2 calculation.

214

Table 12

*Scores of Murderers and Control Brothers on Index of Psychological Frustration **

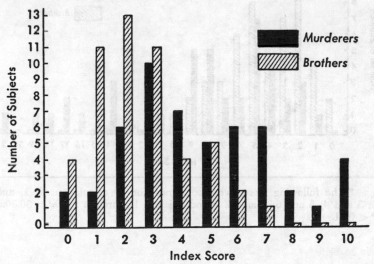

* The following scores were combined for X^2 calculation: 0 and 1; 7, 8, 9, and 10. $X^2 = 22.098$; $P < 0.01$.

Table 13
Scores of Murderers and Control Brothers on Index of
General Frustration *

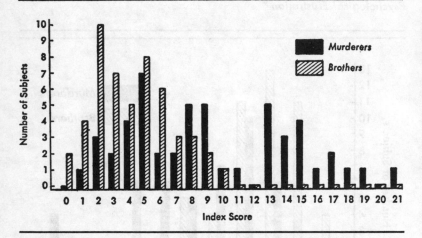

* The following scores were combined for X^2 calculation: 0, 1, and 2; 3 and 4; 5 and 6; 7 and 8; 9 and 10; and 11 through 21. $X^2 = 30.362$; $P < 0.01$.

Table 14
Extent to Which Murderers and Control Brothers Released Anger
in a Reasonable, Verbal Manner at Age 5

	Number of Murderers	Number of Brothers
Usually	4	15
About Half the Time	3	9
Seldom or Never	22	5
Doesn't Apply *	22	22
Total	51	51

$X^2 = 20.072$ $P < 0.01$

* Not included in X^2 calculation.

Table 15

Frequency with Which Murderers and Control Brothers Fought
Physically with Other Children at Age 5

	Number of Murderers	Number of Brothers
Once a Week *	2	1
Once a Month *	7	21
Only Once or Twice **	20	6
Never **	22	20
Unknown ***	0	3
Total	51	51

$$X^2 = 9.134 \qquad P < 0.01$$

* Combined for X^2 calculation.
** Combined for X^2 calculation.
*** Not included in X^2 calculation.

Table 16

Extent to Which Murderers and Control Brothers Dirtied Their
Clothes When "Dressed Up" at Age 5

	Number of Murderers	Number of Brothers
Almost Always *	4	3
Usually *	8	1
About Half the Time	2	10
Occasionally	13	20
Almost Never	24	16
Doesn't Apply **	0	1
Total	51	51

$$X^2 = 12.405 \qquad P < 0.01$$

* Combined for X^2 calculation.
** Never "dressed up." Not included in X^2 calculation.

Table 17

Extent to Which Murderers and Control Brothers Participated in Athletics at Age 17

	Number of Murderers	Number of Brothers
Frequently *	14	23
Occasionally *	13	17
Almost Never **	10	0
Never **	8	11
Unknown ***	6	0
Total	51	51

$$X^2 = 3.858 \qquad P < 0.05$$

* Combined for X^2 calculation.
** Combined for X^2 calculation.
*** Not included in X^2 calculation.

Table 18

Extent to Which Murderers and Control Brothers Went Hunting at Age 17

	Number of Murderers	Number of Brothers
Frequently *	8	5
Occasionally *	8	4
Almost Never **	4	11
Never **	24	29
Unknown ***	7	2
Total	51	51

$$X^2 = 3.816 \qquad P > 0.05$$

* Combined for X^2 calculation.
** Combined for X^2 calculation.
*** Not included in X^2 calculation.

Table 19

Scores of Murderers and Control Brothers on Index of
Acceptable Aggression Release *

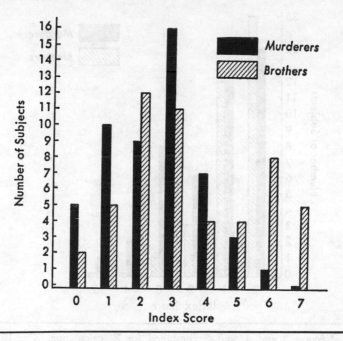

* The following scores were combined for X^2 calculation: 0 and 1;
5, 6, and 7. $X^2 = 13.130$; $P < 0.05$.

Table 20

*Scores of Murderers and Control Brothers on Index of Unacceptable Aggression Release ***

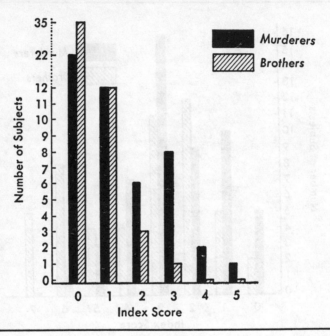

* Scores 3 and 4, and 5 combined for X^2 calculation. $X^2 = 12.298$; $P < 0.01$.

Table 21
Scores of Murderers and Control Brothers on Index of General Aggression Release *

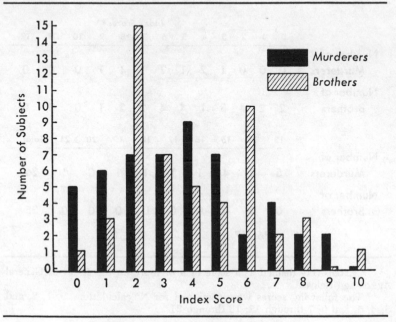

* The following scores were combined for X^2 calculation; 0 and 1; 7, 8, 9, and 10. $X^2 = 13.756$; $P < 0.05$.

Table 22

*Scores on Index of General Frustration of Murderers and Control Brothers Who Employed Aggression Releases Extensively ***

	Index Score: **												
	0	1	2	3	4	5	6	7	8	9	10	11	12
Number of Murderers	0	0	0	1	2	1	2	1	1	1	0	0	0
Number of Brothers	2	2	4	3	1	4	4	2	2	1	0	0	0

	13	14	15	16	17	18	19	20	21	Total
Number of Murderers	5	3	4	1	1	1	1	0	1	26
Number of Brothers	0	0	0	0	0	0	0	0	0	25

$$X^2 = 26.967 \qquad P < 0.01$$

* Extensively defined as a score of 4 or more on the Index of General Aggression Release.

** The following scores were combined for X^2 calculation: 0, 1, 2, and 3; 4, 5, and 6; 7 through 12; 13 through 21.

Table 23

Scores on Index of General Frustration of Murderers and
Control Brothers Who Employed Aggression Release Infrequently *

						Index Score: **					
	0	1	2	3	4	5	6	7	8	9	10
Number of Murderers	0	1	3	1	2	6	0	1	4	4	1
Number of Brothers	0	2	6	4	4	4	2	1	1	1	1

	11	12	13	14	15	16	17	Total
Number of Murderers	1	0	0	0	0	0	1	25
Number of Brothers	0	0	0	0	0	0	0	26

$$X^2 = 7.589 \qquad\qquad P > 0.05$$

* Infrequently defined as a score of 3 or less on the Index of General Aggression Release.
** The following scores were combined for X^2 calculation: 0, 1, and 2; 3 and 4; 5 and 6; 7 through 17.

Appendix B

The Index of Psychological Frustration

Scores for this index were calculated by allotting one point for:

1. Each serious, visible physical defect which was present at birth or developed before the age of twelve years and which persisted one year or longer.

2. "Very rigid" time schedule adhered to by the mother in caring for the child during his first two years. (As opposed to "moderately rigid," "moderately flexible," or "very flexible.")

3. Bottle-fed rather than breast-fed during some portion of the first two months.

4. "Fixed schedule" followed by mother in feeding the child by breast or bottle during the first two months. (As opposed to feeding on a "demand schedule" or a "combination schedule.")

5. Final weaning from breast or bottle started before age of twelve months.

6. Toilet training begun before age of twelve months.

7. Sexual self-play stopped by mother before age of twelve months.

8. Mother responded to child "very often" by crying during first five years of his life. (As opposed to "occasionally" or "never.")

9. Mother responded to child "very often" by isolating herself during first five years of his life. (As opposed to "occasionally" or "never.")

10. Each trauma due to natural events or other individuals, but excluding physical beatings, which occurred before age of twelve years.

11. "Great difficulty" learning to read or "never learned." (As opposed to "moderate difficulty" or "almost no difficulty.")

12. Persistent bedwetting present during preadult years.

13. Stuttering present during childhood.

14. Spent a majority of time playing alone at about age five.

The Index of Acceptable Aggression Release

Scores were calculated by allotting one point for:

1. Verbal loudness at age five classified as loud or average.

2. Anger short of temper tantrums at age five which occurred once a week or more often.

3. Reasonable verbal release of anger at age five which occurred about half the time or more often.

4. Physical fighting at age five once a month or more often.

5. "Talking back" to the mother at age five occasionally or more often.

6. Dirtying clothes when "dressed up" at age five about half the time or more often.

7. Participation in athletics at age seventeen occasionally or more often.

8. Hunting at age seventeen occasionally or more often.

9. Mildly antagonizing others by verbal means at age seventeen occasionally or more often.

The Index of Unacceptable Aggression Release

Scores were calculated by allotting one point for:

1. Lying to the mother at age five frequently or occasionally.

2. Stealing at age five frequently or occasionally.

3. Swearing at age five frequently or occasionally.

4. Temper tantrums which occurred once or more during childhood.

5. Deliberately and seriously hurting animals once or more during childhood or adolescence.

6. Fist fighting once or more at age seventeen.

7. Violent aggression other than fist fighting when intoxicated before age twenty.

Appendix C

"The Cage" * by Joseph T. Galvin

IT was a small, grimy room in a large, dirty, ancient building. There was nothing about it to inspire terror, but only an intensely depressing sensation. There were some features about this room that made it unusual. The door was constructed of steel bars, girded by a heavy lock, quite out of the reach of the tenant. I became that tenant, unwillingly. A Superior Criminal Court, in my home city of Boston, Massachusetts, had passed a sentence of death upon me. Death in the electric chair for a crime that I never committed, yet must pay the full penalty of the law. At the time of my case, the death sentence was mandatory. Death in the electric chair meant exactly that, save in a few extremely rare instances. It was not a comforting sensation to recall that judge intoning the words that meant my days on this earth were now limited to a very few weeks.

I entered that little room about seven-thirty in the evening. My clothes were taken from me and I was subjected to a thorough search of my person that overlooked nothing. Four guards were present, guards there for the express purpose of seeing that no accident could occur that might deprive the state from exacting the due allowed by law. I was stripped to the skin, my toes were spread apart and probed. Fingers were run through my hair to satisfy the searchers that there were no hidden, tiny

* Reprinted with permission of the author and of the editor, *The Tuftonian*.

blades or capsules to utilize in a later suicide attempt. All body orifices were checked, via a rubber glove. I could not have hidden anything though my life were to depend upon it. Those men knew their business thoroughly indeed. Finally they ended their seekings. I was thrown a drab one-piece garment that resembled an old style nightgown and led numbly into the room adjoining.

This room was grimy and dreary and here I would live until I was removed to the earth of some cemetery. I was dazed from the rapidity with which my identity had been taken from me, dazed by the unjust verdict of the court. And I was stunned by the betrayal of those whom I had entrusted with my life, trusted to tell the whole truths, not the snarled mass of half-truths and lies that culminated in my being in the "cage," as I later learned these particular rooms were called. "Death row" was the other title.

When I arrived on that row, there were two other unfortunates awaiting extinction in the electric chair; two men who, like me, would soon take that last long walk, across the prison yard, behind the buildings, and through the little green door that would lead to the end of their, and my, lives as we knew them. Just when we would take that last walk, none of us knew, but we knew in our hearts that it would not be too long away.

Sleep that first night was impossible. I walked about that small room, trying to get tired enough for sleep. It was no use, I was too highly upset by the totally unexpected, unjust verdict of the court. I went back over the trial mentally. Where did the upset come? How? Why should this thing happen to me? In my past life, I had been an alcoholic, even to the point where I was a menace, but only to myself; I was a liability to the public, but never a menace. Why should I be thrown to the wolves? Then the words of one of the men responsible for all this rang in my ears, "Get someone to take this fall, I don't care who, but get someone." They did. I was that someone, and now I must die to keep the records of unsolved crimes from being one higher. What could I do? Money was a thing that never in my entire life did I ever have a sufficient amount of to live comfortably.

Friends? I had few when sober, none when I was drinking. I was alone, and now must die alone.

Musing, and hopelessly mulling over things, I lay there on the cot. I could not sleep, physically I was exhausted, but my mind was not still for a single moment. Like a hare in a closed garden, chased by relentless hounds, my mind raced, raced in vain trying to find the solution to this deadly puzzle. Through the endless night, I sought courage, courage to face what exactly I did not know. The situation looked hopeless.

At last morning came, morning with the blessed light of the new day. Perhaps my court-appointed lawyer would come? Perhaps he could work magic, sort of pull a legal rabbit from his hat, and secure justice for me? I doubted it, but hoped just the same.

After a breakfast of coffee and cigarettes, I received a visit from one of the prison officials, who wanted my life history. I am afraid that I was not very courteous to him, as I was short in my answers to his questions. He reminded me, perhaps unfairly, of the buzzards that hover over a dying creature, and at the moment of death tear chunks of flesh from the still warm carcass. At any rate, I soon disposed of him. Next in the line of official callers was my lawyer. A wonderful, great-souled man, but not a criminal lawyer. He, today, is my best friend. Bert had been a real friend all through the ordeal of the trial, but the cards were stacked against us. Even I, a layman ignorant of the law, could see that clearly. However, he did everything in his power to secure justice for his client. He told me not to despair, that all was not lost. He had appealed the decision to the State Supreme Court. And that it would take quite some time before their answer came back. Saying good-by, for a short while, and bidding me to be of good cheer, Bert left to delve into the law and left me to my meditations.

I sat there, despondent. Then as my nerves gradually settled into a state somewhere near normal, I took stock of the room that was my home, my castle, my all, until I either left it to die in the chair, won a new trial, or was commuted to a life sentence. The exact dimensions of the room were twelve shoe lengths by eight; I should say foot lengths, as I wore no shoes there. There were two tiny windows in a slot in the two-foot solid cement ceiling. These slots were inset about two feet so that you could not under any conditions touch the actual glass itself. Through these slits, I could see a small square of sky about four inches in size. Late in August, I once saw a star! Birds never came near that building for some reason or another.

For lack of better things to do, I counted the pieces of wood in the hard oak flooring. There were 350 pieces of varying lengths; 768 nails held these pieces in place; 99 pieces of steel comprised the barred door. A small chipped and wobbly table and chair were the full extent of my furniture, aside from my cot. The walls were a scabrous, dirty, once yellow-painted surface, dusted with the grime of years, chipped in a thousand places. When it rained, the small windows allowed the wet to blow in; there always was a puddle of water on the floor during a shower. Snow would drift in. It used to puzzle me, why snow and rain could enter so freely, yet no breeze did I ever feel in all the time that I stayed there. It was easy to see that these rooms had never received any attention from the maintenance crews in the past. On the outer side of the barred steel door, a sliding door of wood was so attached that it could be easily slid across the entrance of the room, making me doubly secure. I had two neighbors although I didn't see them for a week; I didn't speak to them for over a month and then it was only in whispers, for talking was forbidden in the "cage." A twenty-four-hour guard was on duty all the time, and nothing could be performed unless it was closely observed by the ever vigilant watcher; the intimate functions of the human in that room were an open book to the men on duty. Five similar cells made the "cage"; and for the first time in many years these cells were soon to be filled by men about to die. Depression and gloom were our constant companions.

We did have one benefit that was denied to most of the other prisoners in the old large prison; we had running water in the cell. A drippy faucet, canted over a stained, filthy toilet bowl, was our sole means of removing the dust and soot that constantly sifted in through the high windows—dust that a thousand near-by locomotives, filthy with the accumulations of coal dust, liberally scattered, and the constant east wind tossed through those small slits, misnamed windows. It was impossible to remain clean.

One week after I was immured in this iron-lined grave, I was told that I was to have a visitor. I ceased my pacing and faced the cell door expectantly, not knowing who the visitor was. Suddenly my vision was almost completely blocked by a dark screen of heavy wire slid across the opening of the doorway. My visitor was there! I could recognize my brother's voice, but could not see him, much less shake his hand. As I peered through the screen, I could see dimly the form of a guard standing at my brother's shoulder, watching the two of us carefully. We talked of home and Mother. I asked my brother, John, how Mom was taking this thing. He replied that she had not given up hope and for me to emulate her in this respect. We had just begun to get used to the wire, when the guard spoke up, "Time up, mister," and John had to leave. He assured me that he would be back the following week to see me. I saw him three years later. I learned that disappointment would always be with me and neglect would soon be a well-known fact in my life.

The next thing that was in line for me was a shower. But before the door was opened the heavy screen was slid out of sight until I should have another visitor. When the door was opened, I was told to come out of the cell and into the tiny corridor. As I did so, an officer stepped behind me and told me to keep walking. I preceded him to a flight of stairs that I didn't remember climbing when I came in to the building and descended one flight. I was then told to turn right and keep on walking until I was told to stop. Far to the rear of the old building was a section called the "flats," "rat alley," and many other peculiar names, all with reason. There I was told to halt. At one side of this section was a small dirty room smelling of crude disinfectant. This was the shower room.

Stripping off the ticking pants and rough shirt that was my entire wardrobe, I stood under the thin trickle of lukewarm water that seeped through the rusty nozzle over my head. There was a bar of yellow laundry soap that I was to use in removing the accumulated grime and sweat of the past week. Rubbing most cautiously, lest I take off more skin than dirt, I somehow managed to get my body clean. The water, never very warm, started to get cold, so I stepped out of the tepid spray, only to be told that I must stay there until the officer with me decided that I was clean enough. The water was now cold, still there was no sound or sign from the guard, so I stepped out again. This time he started to say something, but I guess the bluish tinge to my skin told him to let well enough alone as he signed for me to get dressed. While I had been soaping up, he had very carefully gone through my discarded clothes for anything that might have been utilized as a weapon of defense or offense. He found none.

Leaving the shower gratefully, I started up the short corridor that led through the "flats" to the stairway that led to the "cage." Entering the cell, I saw that my bunk had been pulled away from the wall, the blankets ripped from the bed and tossed on the floor in a tangled mess, the chair turned upside down. It was easy to see that the entire room had been subjected to a thorough search while I was showering below. Well, I thought to myself, you are in prison, and you must expect these things; but still it was disturbing, to say the least. Reaching for a cigarette, I found none, then realized that I must ask the officer for my pack, for he had taken it. Upon asking, I found that we men here were not allowed to have our own smokes in the cell with us. Matches were definitely forbidden, of course. A light would be given if the officer felt like getting up off the comfortable chair he usually sat in for hours at a time. I waited long hours many times in the days to come.

Now that I knew that here I must stay until my fate was finally decided, I realized that I must find something to do with my time. I was very fortunate in that I was allowed plenty of books to read through the long days and interminable nights. Many many times I blessed the good chaplains that brought armloads of books to my cell door. They were all good men.

I set a rigorous schedule for myself to follow each day, and at night I would review the past hours of the day, of that single day, for no other days would I allow in my mind. To try to live for tomorrow was futile and fruitless for me. Who, least of all myself, could foretell if there would be a tomorrow dawning? I never knew what day would be my last on this earth so I tried to live each day as if it were my last. For the good Lord knows that any day could well have been.

I began my day with walking about the room. I figured roughly that about fifty rounds equaled a mile. I made it a rule to do at least two miles a day. This exercise accounted for about two hours a day. Immediately after the last turn was accomplished, I would start a course of setting-up workouts that I had devised myself. These consisted of push-ups, roll-overs, deep-knee bends, and the so-called dynamic tension, which simply meant that I would pit one set of muscles against the other as if I were lifting heavy weights. This I would do for a count of one hundred to five hundred for I had no means of accurately telling time. I tried counting my pulse because I knew that I had a beat of about eighty under normal circumstances. But I had to discard this method as the beat varied with the energy expended. So I would merely count to myself the number of which I set myself. Completing this routine, I would make up my bunk as snugly and as tightly as was humanly possible, then rip it apart to re-make even tighter.

I had such pitifully meager things to occupy my mind that I was forced continually to devise and to improvise in order to pass the weary hours. I would read an entire book, then try to reconstruct the plot. When I had paper, which was very seldom, I kept a daily log. Monotony was my greatest adversary and I battled it with every weapon in my possession. The night officers would bring in the daily paper so I managed to keep abreast of the daily news. I trained myself to a new, a completely new way of life and of looking at life. This may sound easy, but it was the most difficult task of my whole life. Every person on this earth has pleasant memories to reflect upon. I was no exception but the sick realization would hit me: the terribly, the horribly true fact that soon I too would be merely a memory. Also when looking back, I would hurt to know that all was over for me; that never again would I walk with a girl, watch a ball game or play in one, go where I wanted to and when; that never again would I be a free man or even a live man. Realizing that a train of thought along these lines could lead only to insanity, I strove with all my faculties to live this one day at a time.

One day I could handle if it came to me one day at a time. It was up to me to live it thusly. Tomorrow did not exist for me, yesterday was a part of the past that could never be again, and the immediate present was all that I had. I trained myself not to think of what was to come, nor to think back on what was past; today was my day to live. I might be dead tomorrow and the way that it looked, right then, that could happen any time. I never knew when the State Supreme Court would render a verdict or rather a decision. I really had no hopes for a commutation of sentence. I knew that the frame-up foisted on me was a foolproof one, and always despair waited at my elbow for that moment when I would let my mental guard drop. But hope is a flower that grows in the most unlikely of places and in all men at all times. I was no exception—beyond the fact that I lived on hopes more than do most men. I had nothing else.

I wrote to all that I knew but to no avail. I was alone now and alone I must die. The bitter realization of that unjust sentence was like gall but it was all too true. Another crushing blow came when a new warden was appointed. He removed the stoutest weapons from my hands, by curtailing the amount of letters I could send out each week to three. When you are fighting for your life and you must do most of your battling through the medium of letters, that is a terrible blow. You are truly handcuffed. When you are about to die, three letters a week is such a pitiful mite to say what you must say. But that was the way it was.

Exercise was permitted if there was an officer available to take us men into the rear of the prison yard, back to where no one could either see us or talk with us, where we could see no one but the assigned guard. No one must smile a little encouragement. We were the living dead men. Maybe it was just. It is not for me to say; I am merely trying to say what I know and what I felt, condemned to die for a crime I never committed.

When the news came of this wonderful and great thing, this chance to exercise, to walk out in the sun once more—it seemed too good to be true. As subsequent proceedings proved, we were right in our skepticism. There was a joker in the deck! Certainly there was an officer detailed to exercise us men, we walking dead. But, and it was a large but, this man worked five days a week. Two days a week he relieved one officer on the "cage" duty; on two other days he relieved another man, thus deleting four days from our exercise periods. Saturdays, Sundays, and holidays we could not leave the cells. This took care of six days. On the one remaining day, it seemed that even nature leagued against us; we could count on rain. Even if it looked like it might rain, we had to stay inside. This part of the country is not renowned for its aridity. The over-all average for the twenty-five months that I spent in the death cells as far as outside exercise went was twenty minutes a month. The officer detailed to the exercise had to take the men of the punishment block out also and he took them out first, thus further depriving us of any chance for sunlight and air. It was not nice nor was it needful. But that was the way it was.

I entered that cell the twenty-fourth day of October, 1946, and did not leave there until November 17, 1948, when the then-Governor Robert Bradford commuted my sentence of death in the electric chair to life imprisonment. Thus ended my twenty-five months of constant watch and steady confinement. And thus began the life sentence. I am still serving this unearned sentence, dying a little each day, losing a little more hope each day, and still trying to forget the "cage." Please God, one day I will be successful.

Index

APOLLO EDITIONS